Randy Wayne White's
Gulf Coast Cookbook

Also by Randy Wayne White

www.docford.com

Fiction

Sanibel Flats

The Heat Islands

The Man Who Invented Florida

Captiva

North of Havana

The Mangrove Coast

Ten Thousand Islands

Shark River

Twelve Mile Limit

Everglades

Tampa Burn

Dead of Night

Dark Light

Hunter's Moon

Black Widow

Dead Silence

Deep Shadow

Night Vision

Chasing Midnight

Gone (Hannah Smith series)

Night Moves

Deceived (Hannah Smith series)

Nonfiction

*Randy Wayne White's Ultimate Tarpon
    Book* (with Carlene Fredericka Brennen)

Batfishing in the Rainforest

The Sharks of Lake Nicaragua

Last Flight Out

An American Traveler

Tarpon Fishing in Mexico and Florida (an
    introduction)

Fiction (as Randy Striker)

Key West Connection

The Deep Six

Cuban Dead-Lift

The Deadlier Sex

Assassin's Shadow

Grand Cayman Slam

Everglades Assault

Also by Carlene Fredericka Brennen

*Tarpon Tales Lost Stories and Research
    1889–1939* (with Randy Wayne White)

Hemingway in Cuba (with Hilary
    Hemingway)

*Hemingway's Cats: An Illustrated
    Biography*

Hemingway: An Oral Biography (2014)

Writers on Hemingway (2014)

Tarpon Bay on Sanibel Island, Florida

Tarpon Bay Marina

RANDY WAYNE WHITE'S GULF COAST COOKBOOK

With Memories and Photos of Sanibel Island

2nd Edition

Randy Wayne White
and Carlene Fredericka Brennen

with Dr. Dan White

LYONS PRESS
Guilford, Connecticut
An imprint of Globe Pequot Press

Lyons Press is an imprint of Globe Pequot Press.

Project Editor: Lauren Brancato

Text Design: Nancy Freeborn

Layout Artist: Melissa Evarts

Library of Congress Cataloging-in-Publication Data

White, Randy Wayne.
 Randy Wayne White's Gulf Coast cookbook : with memories and photos of Sanibel Island / Randy Wayne White and Carlene Fredericka Brennen with Dr. Dan White. — 2nd edition.
    pages cm
 Summary: "Randy Wayne White's thirteen years as a full-time, light-tackle fishing guide at Tarpon Bay Marina, Sanibel Island, on Florida's Gulf Coast, inspired many of the characters and stories in his New York Times best-selling Doc Ford series. The second edition of Randy Wayne White's Gulf Coast Cookbook pairs more than 125 recipes with photos of the real Tarpon Bay and the most appetizing food-related passages from this acclaimed writer's essays and novels. The result is a veritable memoir of food and adventure, true friends and favorite characters, all in an enjoyable presentation promising satisfying food, drink, and reading"— Provided by publisher.
 Includes index.
 ISBN 978-0-7627-8143-0 (paperback)
 1. Cooking, American—Southern style. 2. Cooking—Gulf Coast (U.S.) 3. Cooking—Florida—Gulf Coast. 4. Sanibel Island (Fla.)—Description and travel. 5. Sanibel Island (Fla.)—Pictorial works. 6. White, Randy Wayne. 7. Food in literature. I. Brennen, Carlene Fredericka. II. White, Dan (Dan L.), Dr. III. Title. IV. Title: Gulf Coast cookbook.
 TX715.2.S68W475 2013
 641.5975—dc23

                                                                                    2013030983

Printed in the United States of America
10 9 8 7 6 5 4 3 2 1

To my North Carolina family, especially Aunt Della, Aunt Jewel,
Aunt JoAnn, Aunt Lucille, Aunt Vera, and Aunt Johnsie, great Southern cooks
all, but the best was my late mother, Georgia Wilson White.
—RWW

To my daughter, Shamie Kelly, a true believer in the preparation of food.
—CFB

Red mangroves,
San Carlos Bay

Tarpon season was always a busy time at the marina during those years; sadly, a fish had to be killed for taxidermy.

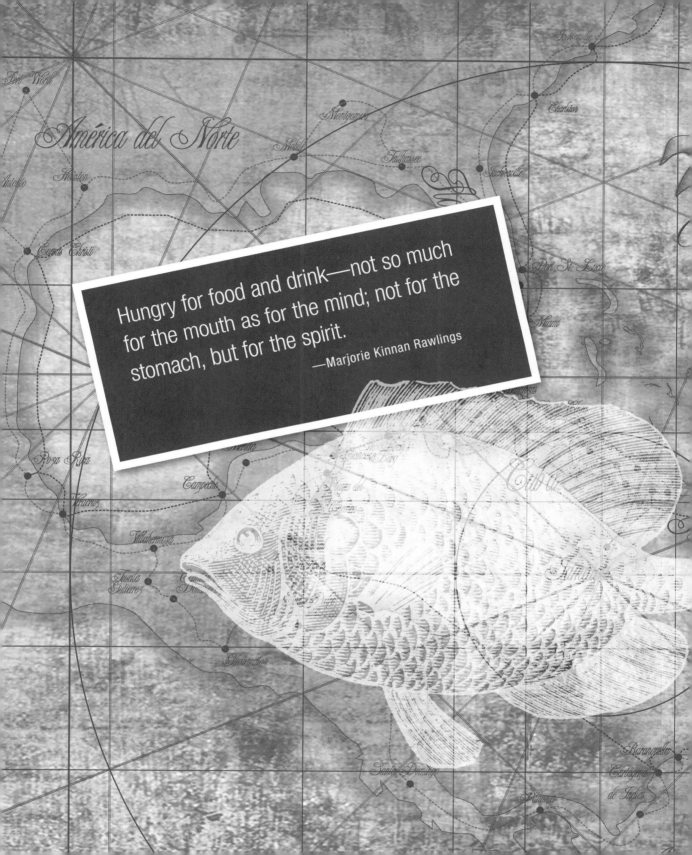

Hungry for food and drink—not so much
for the mouth as for the mind; not for the
stomach, but for the spirit.

—Marjorie Kinnan Rawlings

Black mangroves along the Indigo Trail, J. N. "Ding" Darling National Wildlife Refuge

CONTENTS

Preface xv

Memories of Tarpon Bay xix

  1 Dining with Randy Wayne White 1

  2 Daybreak 7

  3 Appetizers and Snacks 27

  4 Soups, Stews, Chowders, Gazpacho, and Chili 39

  5 Salads 55

  6 Ceviche 63

  7 Herbs 77

  8 Hot Sauces, Salsas, and Chutneys 83

  9 Oysters, Clams, and Mussels 101

10 Shrimp, Crab, and Lobster 115

11 Shark and Other Fish from the Gulf 133

12 Meat and Poultry 149

13 Vegetables, Potatoes, Beans, and Rice 177

14 Outdoor Cooking 197

15 Island Desserts 209

16 Tropical Drinks 225

Afterword 247

Photo Credits 248

Acknowledgments 249

Index 251

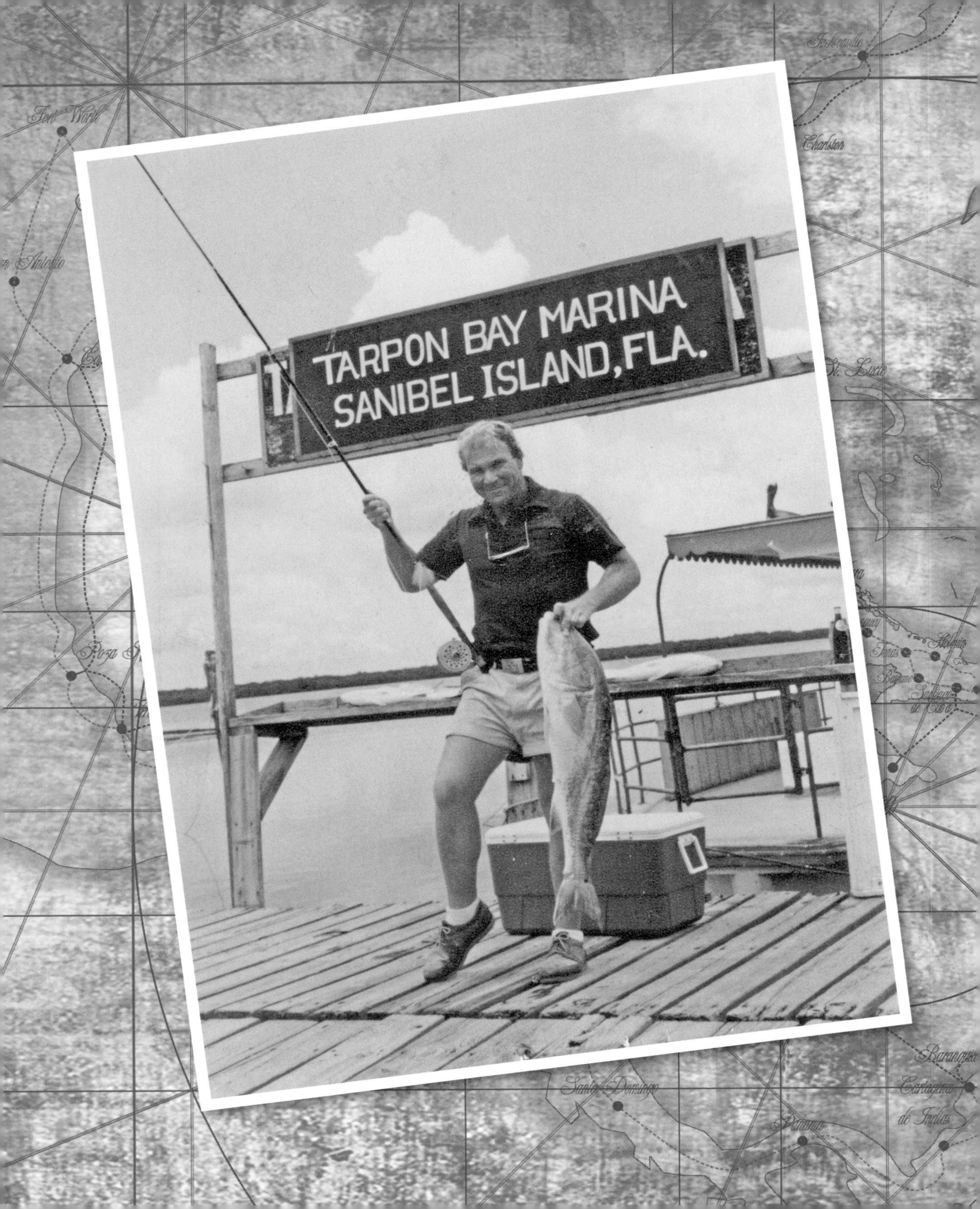
TARPON BAY MARINA
SANIBEL ISLAND, FLA.

PREFACE

In January of 1987, Mack, who ran Tarpon Bay Marina, called a meeting of the fishing guides and told us the feds were closing the bay to powerboat traffic. We had to be out by March.

"The Park Service plans to make a preserve out of Tarpon Bay," he told us. "That means federal employees can live and work here, but we can't."

Because he had to deal with bureaucrats on a daily basis, Mack had a jaundiced view of the breed. One of his favorite lines was, "Take it easy on those guys—there's a reason they work for the government."

After nearly thirteen years making my living as a light-tackle guide, and nearly 3,000 charters, I was out of a job.

I remember feeling surprise, nothing more. Human nature mitigates shock with denial. Tarpon Bay was our home. By virtue of being on the water 300 days a year, fishing every small intersection of grass, mangrove, and sand, we had territorial roots. The bay was *ours*. The government couldn't kick us out.

The government did.

My son Lee was seven, Rogan was five. I was burdened with all the financial obligations typical of self-employed Americans in the late twentieth century: quarterly taxes, a mortgage, car payments, insurance, utilities, plus college savings payments—a wistful luxury, it seemed at the time.

I had to find another job—but what? Aside from my Coast Guard Ocean Operators license and a high school diploma, I wasn't qualified to do anything.

So I wrote a novel, *Sanibel Flats*.

Well . . . that's an oversimplification. I put my boat on a trailer and guided part-time, but I also spent early mornings and late nights at the typewriter doing something I'd always wanted to do—write. I worked relentlessly—worked at learning this demanding craft, determined not to fail the sons and wife I adored . . . and still adore.

My life changed. I became a stay-at-home dad, cleaning and cooking—which was fine with me because I'd always loved to cook. My Deep-South mother believed men should be self-sufficient in the kitchen. I was. With no shortage of seafood, we ate a lot of fish, and I began to collect recipes. That's right—*real* men collect recipes.

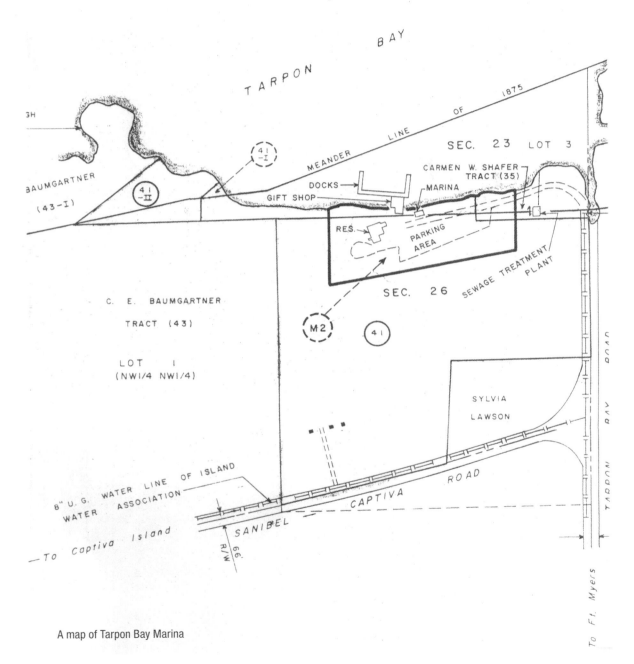

LEE COUNTY, FLORIDA
TALLAHASSEE MERIDIAN

SCALE: 0   300   600   900   1200   FEET

T. 46 S., R. 22 E.

TARPON   BAY

3H

BAUMGARTNER
(43-I)

4 i -I

4 i -II

MEANDER   LINE   OF   1875

SEC.   23   LOT 3

DOCKS

GIFT SHOP

CARMEN W. SHAFER
TRACT (35)

MARINA

RES.

PARKING
AREA

SEC. 26

SEWAGE TREATMENT
PLANT

C. E. BAUMGARTNER

TRACT (43)

M2

41

LOT   1
(NW1/4 NW1/4)

SYLVIA
LAWSON

8" U.G. WATER LINE OF ISLAND
WATER ASSOCIATION

—To Captiva Island

SANIBEL   CAPTIVA   ROAD

R/W
66'

TARPON   BAY   ROAD

To Ft. Myers

A map of Tarpon Bay Marina

Great egret in mangrove forest on Sanibel Island

Outside magazine soon began rewarding my labors at the typewriter with assignments to such far-flung places as Vietnam, Borneo, Australia, Cuba, Africa, and Central and South America. My collection of recipes grew, and so did my passion for cooking, as well as a new hobby—collecting hot sauces and growing chili peppers. It was on a trip to Cartagena, Colombia, that I met commercial chili grower Jorge Araujo, who was distraught because many hectares of his commercial pepper plants had accidentally cross-pollinated with wild chilies. The resulting pepper was wonderfully fragrant and pungent but not saleable to megacorporations such as Tabasco. Giorgio made the brave decision to produce his own sauce, and the results were extraordinary. The sauces tasted so good, I risked $5,000 from our slim bank account and imported a custom red sauce and a custom green sauce under my own label. I had no idea where, how, or if I could sell them.

They sold. Within a few months, I had to reorder.

Writing remains my life's work and passion, but I'm still importing hot sauces. I am now involved with three great restaurants, including Doc Ford's Sanibel Rum Bar & Grille, my first with award-winning flavors from the Caribbean Rim. I also have another location, Doc Ford's Fort Myers Beach Rum Bar & Grille, a marvelous waterfront location on Matanzas Pass, and my newly opened Doc Ford's Captiva Rum Bar & Grille on beautiful Captiva Island. Fishing, writing, and food—not a bad combination. Enjoy! Visit us online at www.docfords.com.

—*Randy Wayne White*

After a good day of big game fishing

MEMORIES
OF TARPON BAY

At the good marinas around Florida, the old and important traditions die hard. —*Captiva*, RWW

Tarpon Bay was a type of marina once known in the South as a "fish camp," which is to say the facility was long established, the bay was shallow, buildings were sun-bleached, and the docks were wobbly. Also, the marina sold fish—fresh, cooked, and frozen. Out back of the marina office, where mangroves shaded the water, there was a commercial scale and a cleaning table. Pelicans and egrets liked to stand on that table, waiting for handouts.

Tarpon Bay was not like the concrete and corrugated marinas preferred by government code-enforcers—which is probably why it was such a popular place. Dockage for small boats could be had at a price, and there was a waiting list. Joyce, the deep-fry cook, made the best conch sandwich on the islands, so at lunchtime, the traffic in the dusty parking lot was as noisy as the patrons were enthusiastic. Because Tarpon Bay Marina looked the way it looked—crooked docks, the bay, small boats, mangroves, and bleached wood—it attracted artists, too; artists not just of the heart, but also of the hand and the eye. These artists would set up their easels on the docks, mix their paints, and try to capture the look of the place. A very few actually captured the feel of the place; a rare occurrence that drew personal congratulations even from the marina's fishing guides—not that we fishing guides were snobs, or even stingy with praise. It was just that, to congratulate anyone, we had to leave our shady lunch spots. Spend 300 days a year on the water, in the Florida sun, and your standards in art will sharpen even if your appreciation for art does not.

Tarpon Bay Marina did have its own feel. All good marinas do—and there are fewer and fewer good marinas. A good marina comprises more than the sum of its docks, bait tanks, and ship's store. A marina is an ephemeral community as intricately linked as any coral colony, and with a personality flavored, more or less, by each of the individuals who form it. Some marinas are as friendly as stray dogs, some are grumpy and aggressive, and some are as uninteresting as the corporations

(Clockwise from top) Tarpon Bay Marina office and seafood market. Marina owner, Mack. Nick at the marina's front desk. I may have been talking to my publisher.

that own them. You would have to ask a Tarpon Bay client how friendly we were, but I can say for certain that the marina was never uninteresting.

Tarpon Bay Marina was dominated by its proprietor, Mack. Mack was a big man partial to Cuban cigars and plantation hats, and he did everything with bold strokes and a capitalistic flourish. Mack made a lot of money as a banker, retired when banking lost its charm, and took a flyer on a marina. "Where free enterprise is just a little freer," Mack was fond of saying.

He loved money—no, he loved the rituals involved with making money. Offer Mack a chance to bargain, an opportunity to dicker, and he would drop even the most compelling task to try and beat you down a dollar or two. Oh hell, Mack did love money. He didn't lie about it, and I shouldn't either. Hundreds of times in the years that I was at the marina, Mack looked up from the ringing cash register, winked, and said, "They're playing my song."

Mack was a good businessman, but he was more than that too. Mack had hobbies. He enjoyed gambling and fishing, and he dabbled in antiques and art. He collected paintings of clowns—everyone on the island knew that. But what few knew was that Mack's collection of clowns extended into his own work corps. If you were a plain, honest, hardworking lug, you didn't have much chance of being hired by Mack. But if you had some personality quirk, if your interests ranged beyond snook fishing, if your sense of humor was more liberal than your politics—then Mack probably had a job for you. Among the personalities who made up the marina community were Willie, an eighty-year-old German refugee, whose bad temper was exacerbated by low blood pressure and a stint in the Nazi youth corps; Graeme, who left his New Zealand home at sixteen to travel the world before settling on Sanibel where, for many years, he wooed a fascinating variety of women and worked—despite the fact that he was in the country illegally; and Nick, who was smart and hardworking, but who stuttered so badly that he was incomprehensible on the telephone.

So what did Mack do?

He put Willie in charge of the rental boats, which meant that, on a daily basis, Willie dealt with dozens of amateur boaters under the most maddening of circumstances. "Mister!" we could hear Willie yell from the docks at some bewildered rookie, "Don't aim dah damn motor, steer it! It's a boat, not a gun!"

He put Nick in charge of answering the phone in the fish market. Invariably, the caller's first question was about variety, and we would all hold our breath while Nick replied by rote, "Grouper, sna-na-napper, flounder, sea trout, cah-cah-cobia, shark, and . . . da-dol-dah-da-dol-do-dol . . . maui maui."

He made Graeme (the illegal alien) marina manager, which meant that it was Graeme's responsibility to deal with all the petty, self-important government officials that a marina invariably attracts.

Graeme had roamed the world and knew many things, so ineffectual bureaucrats were hardly a challenge. Mack loved the irony of that, relished the private knowledge that the same people who would have scrambled to have Graeme deported (had they only known) were not in Graeme's intellectual ballpark. "Take it easy on them," Mack would say kindly. "There's a reason they work for the government."

Tarpon Bay Marina was not a mean-spirited place; indeed, it was usually amiable and always cordial. But if you could not laugh at yourself, it was not a place to linger. When Mack was once bested in a business deal, we began calling him "Top Dollar," for he had paid top dollar for some piece of junk. He loved the nickname, and he always smiled a little when he heard it, so we called him that for years. Among the marina family, Nick was not embarrassed about his stutter, and we all pulled openly for him when he was on the phone. Year by year he became more confident so, on those occasions when he informed a caller, "And we have da-dah-dol-da-dah . . . DOLPHIN," the caller probably wondered why there was wild applause in the background.

As for Willie, his humor never much improved—but then, no one really expected it to.

We fishing guides certainly weren't spared. Young guides are prone to haughtiness so, to keep us in our places, Mack would sometimes tell new clients outlandish stories of what they could expect to catch with us—and then laugh at their dejected expressions when we returned with fourteen-inch sea trout instead of the blue marlin and giant tuna he had promised (but that do not frequent the waters around Sanibel Island).

During my years at Tarpon Bay, I was also trying to be a writer, which Mack and Graeme and the rest well knew, so they offered encouragement when they could. Fishing guides are not easy to get in touch with. We are usually out netting bait before first light, fishing until noon, back on the water at one, and not finished at the cleaning table until well after five. At a busy marina, that is the schedule—and I sometimes fished that schedule for more than forty consecutive days without pause. Which is good for a guide, but bad for a writer, because editors cannot call you when you are in a boat chasing fish. So the few editors who were interested in my work made it a point to call the marina during my lunch hour.

On those rare occasions when they called, Mack or Graeme would unfailingly page me over the public-address system, even though I was right outside the door. I'm sure the editors heard them: "Paging Captain White, Captain Randy White, you have another damn call from New York," which was a kind attempt to make me sound more important—and more in demand—than I actually was. When I received that page, I did not tarry—and not just because I was desperate for

(Clockwise from top) The back docks, scale and cleaning table at the marina. Marina manager, Graeme. Filleting a fifty-pound black drum fish for my charter.

Nick and I weigh in a tarpon at the scale. The big fish was to be mounted.

writing jobs, though I was. I hustled in because once, when I lingered, I arrived at the marina office to hear Mack telling an important editor, "Randy's not going to cover the America's Cup for you or anybody else until he gets these goddamn mullet gutted."

I worked Tarpon Bay Marina as a fishing guide for nearly eleven years, several thousand charters. And I would probably be guiding there still if a few low-rung bureaucrats hadn't decided to close the marina not only to powerboats, but also to fishing guides.

Never mind that most guides don't tear up grass flats because they rarely go aground. Never mind that most guides are fanatical about game laws. Never mind that most fishing guides put on a daily workshop on the proper way to release fish—a tutorial that pyramids through all fishing society via our clients. The bureaucrats, even though they were trying to do their best, couldn't understand this and, in the end, it didn't matter.

As Mack would say, "Take it easy on them. There's a reason they work for the government."

It's been a couple of years since the marina closed, but the influence it exerted on our lives is still felt by most of us. Graeme has sailed on to the Virgin Islands, where he finds the massive charter operation he runs almost as challenging as the name of the region in which he lives. Nick still stutters, but he does so as a confident young father and manager of a successful business. The other Tarpon Bay fishing guides, Alex and Neville, are busier than ever working out of a neighboring marina.

But not all of us are still around to feel the influence of Tarpon Bay. Willie passed away without once making peace with a rental boat operator—not that anyone really expected him to. What we also didn't expect was that Mack, during a night of wagering at the greyhound races, would suffer a massive heart attack and die. But he did. The only thing about it that wasn't surprising was that Mack went out a big winner, payoffs on a couple of rich trifectas folded lovingly in his money clip.

So what does all this have to do with my work and food? In high school, most of us learned that astronomers, by calculating the paths of known bodies, could deduce the existence of unknown and unseen planets. Well, in my books, Tarpon Bay Marina is the unseen planet; the molding gravitational force that may not have shaped the stories, but uncertainty had an influence. More than one of these pieces was finished in a rush at 5:00 a.m. so that I could get it into the mailbox and then hustle to the marina to start catching bait for the day's charter. More than one of these pieces arrived in Chicago or New York with the grease stains from one of Joyce's conch sandwiches still fresh on it.

(Clockwise from top) Marina owner Mack and boat manager Willie. The marina's seafood market always offered plenty of freshly caught shrimp and whatever fish was in season. Joyce made a conch sandwich and chowder that I still think about today.

The marina also provided me with my biggest advantage as a traveler; no matter where I went, no matter who I encountered (or what marvelous foods I discovered), I could introduce myself as a fishing guide and enjoy a warmer welcome than most writers could expect—or deserve. People naturally trust and empathize with a fisherman. I don't know why that is true, but it is. People quite rightly think that a guy who would travel halfway around the world in search of a fish—a fish he probably won't catch anyway—not only deserves their help, but, by God, requires it.

—*Batfishing in the Rainforest,* RWW

(Left) Nick displays a mixed bag of fish, including a nice size cobia. (Right) A quiet morning at Tarpon Bay

Cooking lobster on the grill

CHAPTER 1

DINING WITH RANDY WAYNE WHITE

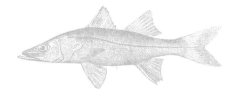

"Breaking bread" draws you into the family and their realm of reality. It is a universal sign of initial acceptance and friendship. —RWW

Food is something that is a given in the lives of those of us lucky enough to have been born and raised in a time and land of plenty. I can still remember the smell of my Southern mom's fried chicken, her green beans with bacon and onion, and small red potatoes cooking to the appropriate tenderness, with a background of baking homemade biscuits and sweet rolls. It was Sunday dinner, a tradition in my family and that of most other families raised in the '50s. Unfortunately, this time with family and friends is increasingly rare in our age of computers, video games, satellite television, cell phones, and measuring by gigabytes, megabytes, and gigahertz. E-mail has even taken away the pleasure of hearing a loved one's voice, much less enjoying their company at a meal. A meal together is where the day and week can be discussed, differences amicably ironed out, and plans made for the evening, next day, next month, or next year.

Sharing food brings those who do it closer as human beings. It provides a chance to give and receive, a chance to notice body language, to glance at everyone seated around the table, to illustrate our feelings and intentions to each other. A meal with others is a time when we show, even silently, affection and attention to those whom we otherwise tend to take for granted, or to those we have just met. A time for peace, reflection, and planning. My mother was a fabulous cook! As the second oldest of ten children and born in a poor Southern family, she left school after the fourth grade to help her mother raise her newer brothers and sisters while her father took care of the livestock, fields, and garden that provided almost all of the family's food. Food was eaten fresh, canned for cooler and leaner times, or smoked and brined to preserve meats against the Southern heat. Refrigeration then, as in many tropical countries now, was unavailable or rare. Small animals such as rabbits, chickens, squirrels, and fish were eaten before they could spoil. But the larger protein sources, beef and pork, were smoked. I can still smell the smokehouse filled with hams, bacon, and strips of "jerked beef." Beef and even chicken were canned for preservation, and the "fatback" or "salt pork" of butchered pigs was salted away.

My father genuinely loved my mother's cooking, especially the Sunday and holiday meals. And she could bake; my gosh, did she bake! One year, she gave away more than fifty "Russian tea rings" to friends and many of my dad's patients. The Amish patients were particularly appreciative, as they seemed more aware of all the work that went into making them. She made pies from fresh fruit with lard or solid Crisco crusts, "popovers," cinnamon sweet rolls, breads, and, of course, there were the cakes. Two layers, three layers, seven-layer cakes in chocolate, white, or yellow. Then there was the frosting! My favorite is still the "seven-minute frosting"—a soft, light, creamy, yet not-too-sweet white cloud of a topping spread over multiple layers of cake, plain or coconut or caramel, with nuts and maraschino cherries.

She passed away in 1991 taking all of her cooking secrets with her. Of course she said she had none—"just a pinch of this and a little of that," she'd say. I never saw my mom use a cookbook. Unfortunately, I didn't inherit her talent, and I keep recipes, however rudimentary, of the dishes or methods I am particularly fond of— and occasionally, I even use them!

My dad—a 101st Airborne Paratrooper, with rare "Glider" wings, met my mother during World War II while he was in training at Fort Bragg, North Carolina. She was working as a cashier in the "PX" and swept him off his feet with her good looks, charm, and a strength I've only ever found in true Southern women. It's an iron-fist-in-a-velvet-glove trait that my dad found irresistible. After a whirlwind romance, he made the mistake of marrying my mother without getting my grandfather's permission.

Mom and her older sister had a strict curfew of ten o'clock, no exceptions— none—period. Well, on the day my folks decided to get married, my mom was twenty-one and my dad was barely twenty-one. They arrived back at her home one half hour after curfew, only to be greeted by my grandfather. Before they had a chance to explain their tardiness, Grandpa sent his 101st Airborne "Screaming Eagle," beating feet with one slow, deep-throated, drawled sentence: "Son—if you

This giant tarpon was mounted by my charter. Today, most tarpon aren't killed for trophies or mounts, but are released to catch another day.

ever bring my daughter home this late again, I'll shoot you down in the street like a dog." I never did learn how they eventually broke the news they were married—but they did, and it lasted more than forty years.

Dad never got fat, but he ate damn well. He was particularly fond of my mom's Southern fried chicken. (See "Georgia Wilson White's North Carolina Fried Chicken" on page 161 for a recipe as close as I, or any of my aunts, could come to the real thing.) And he loved the way she prepared creamed onions. (That recipe, as close as possible, is also provided on page 186.)

His eyes would light up, and he would announce the specialty to the rest of us with delight. There wasn't always a lot of money, but thanks to my mother, we never went hungry or had a meal that didn't taste fit for a king.

A huge bright spot in my travels has been being invited to share the food—however simple or scarce—of the wonderful people I've met. "Breaking bread" draws you into their family and their realm of reality.

It is a universal sign of initial acceptance and friendship. Being touched by a stranger's faith is not uncommon for an American traveler. Neither is being asked to share the food and company of many newly made friends while fishing in out-of-the-way places. It is part of the adventure-travel experience. The borders of that experience are limited only by one's disinclination to get off one's duff and try something, anything, new. A careful, monotonous life, in its way, is predacious. It feeds upon that singular human spark in all of us which is brave-hearted and unique. Personally, I'd rather swim with sharks. There are far darker, far more sinister things out there cruising.

In hot climates—especially in many of the tropical countries and islands we tend to seek out for their beauty and the adventure they may offer—it is not considered rude to ask to inspect the kitchen, and the vegetable and meat products you may be eating from the "menu." If you embarrass your travel partners with this request, then you are traveling with neophytes or need new travel companions. You will be the one enjoying your trip and eating experiences while they are at the pharmacia trying to remedy their self-inflicted gastrointestinal misery.

I was lucky enough to learn this early on from the son of a very wealthy and famous Eastern family who had travel experience far beyond my own. We had met by chance on a small Caribbean island where we had both sought solace and solitude and a few days to heal from the abrasions of life. We sat in a dirt-floor, thatched-roof cantina with dogs, children, and chickens running through, chasing or being chased, in and out of screenless doorways. While reviewing the chalkboard on the wall that listed the day's offerings and prices, he said, "Hey, you do want to look at the kitchen and food with me before we order, don't you?" My first thought was, "How could I embarrass the owners of this little establishment?

They were a very nice couple with the children, dogs, and chickens who were our other dinner companions. But my new friend asked me this question as he was already heading toward the cooking area, so I followed and learned an invaluable lesson about eating in a world that does not (or cannot) abide by the food-quality rules that so many of us take for granted.

The rule "If you can't peel it, boil it, or open it, don't eat it" is not a bad one, but it is one that will deprive you of experiencing the smells, tastes, and satisfaction gained by eating local foods with old friends and new acquaintances.

My good friend and fellow author, Peter Matthiessen, is a Zen Buddhist monk, and he tells me Buddha said, "There is no joy in eating alone." And it's true. Try to enjoy food with as many people as you can. Share the recipes in this book, and you will be opening the door to friendships that may last you a lifetime!

—Dr. Dan White & Randy Wayne White

Getting ready for my morning charter

CHAPTER 2

DAYBREAK

There is a weight to the early morning hours;
a palpable density that's a little like being
underwater. You can feel the press of it on your
shoulders, the pressure of it in your inner ear.
The resonance of one's own heartbeat is the test
of silence—a fragile, fragile sound. —*Captiva,* RWW

The Early Morning Hour

Because morning was his favorite time, Tucker Gatrell was up before everybody. All his life, it had been that way. Tuck put coffee to the fire and added a handful of chicory for body. Outside, birds made their tentative first twitterings from the hush of jasmine and poinciana, and in the autumnal darkness the wind was freshening from off the bay, smelling of open sea and far islands. When the coffee was ready, he carried his mug to the porch, propped his boots on the railing, scratched [the dog] Gator's ears to make sure he was there, then settled himself in that quiet time to watch the landscape change.

In the east, there was no sun, but an orange corona boiled over the horizon, throwing shards of westwarding light. The sky was a fragile lemon-blue, translucent as a pearl, and clouds over the Gulf absorbed the light in towering peaks, fiery like snow glaciers about a dark sea. Birds flying—Tuck could see their gray shapes closing. A formation of ibis—curlew, he thought of them—glided across the bay and were briefly illuminated, combusting into brilliant plumes that produced an ethereal white light. Then the birds banked into shadow, silent as falling stars, and were gone.

Tucker watched them, feeling a strange sense of loss and a curious ache, like nostalgia. He finished his coffee, then leaned to get at the foil pouch of Red Man in his back pocket as morning spread itself into graduated light, from dusk to pearl to pale green-blue.

"Don't that air smell sweet!" Talking aloud, though no one was around to hear but the dog.

—*The Man Who Invented Florida,* RWW

Early morning light at
Mantanzas Pass

Apricot-Raisin Granola

This recipe comes from Carlene's good friend, Lynda Leonard-Boyce. Lynda and her husband Ken are past owners of the popular island restaurant, the Sanibel Café. If your family or friends are granola lovers, why not make your own? Try this one. —RWW

5 cups old-fashioned oats, uncooked

⅓ cup finely packed brown sugar

½ cup wheat germ

⅓ cup canola oil

¼ cup honey

¼ teaspoon almond extract

1 cup raisins, regular or golden

1 cup chopped dried apricots

Preheat oven to 350°F. Place oats in an ungreased 13 × 9-inch baking pan and heat in the oven for 10 minutes to toast. Place toasted oats, brown sugar, and wheat germ in a large bowl. Add canola oil, honey, almond extract, raisins, and apricots. Toss to mix until ingredients are well coated.

Transfer mixture to the ungreased baking pan and bake, stirring frequently, for 15 to 20 minutes or until granola is golden brown.

Remove granola from oven and cool in the pan. Stir until crumbly. Place granola in an airtight container and refrigerate until needed.

SERVES 8.

Recipe courtesy of Ken Boyce and Lynda Leonard-Boyce.

Brazilian Tuna Omelet

Mal Assado (mahlah-SAH-doh)

This is a great dish to serve with one or more of my Walden Pond Bloody Marys (page 228).
—RWW

3 eggs, separated

1 tomato, seeded and chopped

2 tablespoons chopped green bell pepper

2 tablespoons chopped onion

1 (6½ ounce) can tuna, drained

salt and pepper

2 tablespoons canola oil

Place egg yolks in a small bowl. Beat with a wire whisk. Set aside. Place tomato, bell pepper, onion, and tuna in a medium bowl. Stir to mix well. Season with salt and pepper to taste. Add beaten egg yolks and stir to combine.

Place egg whites in the large bowl of an electric mixer. Beat until whites are stiff but not dry. Using a spatula or wooden spoon, gently fold tomato mixture into beaten egg whites.

Place a large skillet over medium heat. Add 2 tablespoons of oil to skillet. When oil is hot, add egg mixture. Cook until underside is golden. Using 2 spatulas, gently turn omelet over. Cook until underside is golden. Serve Mal Assado along with rice and beans and a green salad.

SERVES 2.

Recipe courtesy of Randy Wayne White.

Broiled Florida Grapefruit

An unusual combination of tropical and Southern cooking. —RWW

2 large grapefruit, cut in half

4 tablespoons butter

½ cup plus 2 teaspoons sugar

2 tablespoons cinnamon

4 sautéed chicken livers

Preheat broiler. Using a grapefruit or paring knife, loosen sections of each half-grapefruit. Cut a small hole in the center of each half. Place 1 tablespoon butter in each hole.

Place ½ cup sugar and the cinnamon in a small bowl and stir to mix well. Sprinkle each half-grapefruit with 2 tablespoons of the cinnamon-sugar mixture. Place grapefruit on a shallow-rimmed baking sheet. Place baking sheet on oven rack positioned

4 inches from broiler. Broil 8 to 10 minutes, or just until grapefruit tops are lightly browned and bubbling.

Remove baking sheet from oven. Place a chicken liver in the center of each half-grapefruit. Sprinkle each half with ½ teaspoon sugar. Return sheet to oven rack and broil 2 more minutes. Serve immediately.

SERVES 4.

Recipe courtesy of Randy Wayne White.

Pecan Pie Muffins

My Aunt Della Wilson Denson considered this recipe, a muffin for all occasions and was always a crowd pleaser at family brunches. —RWW

    1 cup of brown sugar, packed

    ½ cup all-purpose flour

    ¼ teaspoon baking powder

    1 cup pecans, chopped

    ⅔ cup butter, melted

    2 eggs, beaten

Combine brown sugar, flour, baking powder, pecans and set aside. Use a whisk to combine melted butter, eggs and mix well. Stir all together until moistened. Put in paper-lined muffin pans. Fill cup ⅔ full. Bake for 30 minutes at 350°F until light brown. Cool before eating.

MAKES 12 MUFFINS.

Recipe courtesy of Randy Wayne White.

Della Wilson Denson

Captiva Cool

An island favorite for breakfast, brunch, or lunch. Serve with your favorite muffins and fresh fruit. —RWW

   2 tablespoons margarine

   6 large eggs

   4 ounces cream cheese, softened

   ½ cup chopped scallions

Place a large skillet over medium-low heat. Add margarine. Place eggs in a small mixing bowl. Beat with a wire whisk. When margarine has melted, add beaten eggs, cream cheese, and scallions to skillet. Cook egg mixture, stirring constantly to scramble, until eggs are cooked through. Serve with muffins and fruit.

SERVES 2 TO 3.

Recipe courtesy of Mike Billheimer of The Lighthouse Café on Sanibel Island.

Favorite Beer Muffins

Yes, beer is a food. It can also be a delicious breakfast. —RWW

   1 tablespoon margarine

   2 cups biscuit mix of choice

   ¾ cup favorite beer

   1 tablespoon granulated natural cane sugar

Preheat oven to 400°F. Grease muffin tins with margarine. Place biscuit mix, beer, and sugar in a large bowl. Stir vigorously with a wooden spoon until batter is smooth. Fill each muffin tin three-quarters full. Bake 12 to 15 minutes or until a toothpick inserted in the center comes out clean.

MAKES 6 MUFFINS.

Recipe courtesy of Randy Wayne White.

It was a powder-blue morning, summer-slick but with a September horizon. The meld of sea and sky created a translucent sphere into which I seemed to be traveling at speed: a liquid void on which floated dark islands that were as solitary as I. —*Ten Thousand Islands*, RWW

Sunrise at Sanibel Lighthouse Beach

Nayrilla's Corn Bread

My grandmother Nayrilla Wilson like most Southern women of their time made their corn bread crusty and with little or no sugar. That is why the sugar in her recipe is listed as optional. I myself am a traditionalist. —RWW

 1 cup cornmeal

 1 tablespoon baking powder

 1 cup self-rising flour

 2 eggs

 2 tablespoons corn oil

 1 cup buttermilk

 2 tablespoons of sugar (optional)

Mix together in large bowl cornmeal, baking powder and flour. In a separate bowl beat eggs, corn oil and buttermilk. Add dry ingredients and stir until blended. Pour batter into an 8-inch square, greased pan. Bake 20–25 minutes at 350°F or until firm when pressed. Serve warm.

SERVES 9.

Recipe courtesy of Randy Wayne White.

Nayrilla Wilson

Mexican Tomato Poached Eggs

Huevos ahogados (way-vohss), meaning drowned eggs, is one of my favorite breakfast recipes. It tastes especially great after a late-night party and served with one of my Doc Ford's Captiva Sunrise cocktails—my version of a Bloody Mary, with rum (page 231)—this meal will get your motor running. —RWW

    2 tablespoons olive oil

    1 onion, chopped

    1 clove garlic, minced

    1 teaspoon dried oregano

    2 teaspoons dried parsley

    salt and pepper

    1 teaspoon chili powder

    2 green bell peppers, seeded and chopped

    1½ cups canned tomatoes, drained with juice reserved

    3 jalapeño or serrano chile peppers, seeded and chopped (optional)

    4 eggs

    2 to 3 cups cooked rice

    Doc Ford's Green Flash Hot Sauce (available at www.docford.com)

Place a large skillet over medium heat and add oil. When oil is hot, add onions, garlic, oregano, and parsley. Sauté, stirring occasionally, about 3 minutes or until onions are translucent. Add salt, pepper, and chili powder to taste.

Add bell peppers, tomatoes, and hot peppers. Sauté, stirring occasionally, about 3 minutes or until peppers are tender.

Add reserved tomato juice. Bring to a boil. Gently crack eggs atop tomato mixture. Poach eggs for 3 minutes or until cooked through. Serve each poached egg atop a serving of rice. Top each egg with an equal amount of vegetable mixture. Sprinkle each serving with a few drops of my hot sauce.

SERVES 4.

Recipe courtesy of Randy Wayne White.

[O]ne of the earth's few unique ecosystems—Florida's River of Grass—actually begins on the outskirts of Orlando. "The real magic kingdom." —*Dead of Night*, RWW

Sanibel Island Lighthouse

Sanibel Seafood Benedict with Alfredo Sauce

Owner Mike Billheimer was raised on Sanibel Island, and his charming restaurant, The Lighthouse Café, is a local favorite. Located within walking distance of the island's historic lighthouse, the restaurant's delicious food and friendly staff make the café a pleasant place to dine. —RWW

1 large croissant, split in half lengthwise

2 tablespoons butter or margarine

1 cup sliced broccoli florets

½ cup sliced mushrooms

2 ounces scallops

4 ounces cooked shrimp, shelled and deveined

2 ounces cooked crab leg meat, rinsed, drained, and picked over

½ teaspoon minced garlic

½ teaspoon thyme

Alfredo Sauce:

1 cup heavy cream

½ teaspoon minced garlic

pinch of thyme

½ cup grated Parmesan cheese

2 eggs

Toast croissant halves until light brown. Place a large skillet over medium heat. Add butter or margarine and heat until melted. Add broccoli and mushrooms. Sauté until vegetables are tender and all liquid has been absorbed.

Meanwhile, place scallops in a small saucepan with a little water. Bring to a simmer over medium heat, cover, and cook for 2 minutes. Drain scallops.

Add scallops, shrimp, crab, ½ teaspoon garlic, and ½ teaspoon thyme to vegetable mixture and cook until heated through.

Meanwhile, place cream in a small saucepan. Place pan over low heat and bring to a simmer. Add ½ teaspoon minced garlic and a pinch of thyme. Mix with a wire whisk. Slowly add Parmesan cheese, whisking continuously until sauce thickens.

Place an inch of water in a medium skillet over medium heat. Bring to a light boil. Crack eggs into water, taking care not to break the yokes. Using a spoon, douse egg with water until egg whites form.

To assemble: Place a croissant half on each of two dinner plates. Place half the seafood mixture atop each croissant. Top seafood mixture with a poached egg. Ladle Alfredo Sauce over Seafood Benedict. Serve immediately.

SERVES 2.

Recipe courtesy of Mike Billheimer, The Lighthouse Café on Sanibel Island.

A reddish egret in Tarpon Bay

There was a dazzling blue day through the window, with smoky thunderheads forming beyond the marina. The cloud towers were motionless, tinged with pink and purple, so they seemed as permanent as an Arizona canyonscape. —*Ten Thousand Islands*, RWW

Jams, Jellies, and Marmalades

Jane Arnett's Island Marmalades and Jellies

"Canning marmalades and jellies on Useppa is great fun. From our kitchen I stare out at our sailboat bobbing on its mooring or hear the owl hooting from the banyan tree both day and night. For years I have been giving homemade jellies, jams, and marmalade for Christmas gifts. I use the basic Ball Canning Jar Recipes. For my fruit I use Useppa gleanings only, whatever I can find on the ground. Key limes and sour oranges work best. Chopping the fruit in the blender with water will make a super marmalade. Canning is a labor of love. I usually have 3 very large pots going on my stove: one for the fruit mixture, one holding just sterilized (boiled for 20 minutes) jars, and a third to process the finished sealed jars." —Jane Arnett

3½ cups juice or chopped fruit

water as needed

6 cups sugar

cinnamon

ginger

nutmeg

1 package Certo pectin

Place juice or fruit, water, and sugar in a large pot over medium-high heat. Bring to a roaring boil that cannot be stirred down, stirring constantly to keep sugar from burning. Add a smidgen of cinnamon, ginger, and nutmeg to taste. Add Certo and keep stirring for 1 minute. Skim off any white foam that remains. Pour into sterilized pint canning jars and put on lids. Process in a boiling-water bath for 12 minutes to prevent spoiling and ensure freshness. (Do not double recipe; make each batch individually.)

MAKES APPROXIMATELY 5 TO 6 PINTS.

Recipe courtesy of Jane Arnett, Useppa Island.

Watermelon Jam

Every Southerner should have a recipe for watermelon jam. This is mine. —RWW

4 cups watermelon, seeded and mashed

¼ cup lemon juice

¼ teaspoon ground ginger

1 package dried fruit pectin

5½ cups sugar

3 (1-pint) canning jars with flat lids, sterilized

Place watermelon, lemon juice, ginger, and fruit pectin in a large saucepan over high heat. Bring to a full, rolling boil, stirring constantly. Quickly add sugar. Return mixture to a full, rolling boil, stirring constantly, for 1 minute. Remove saucepan from heat and ladle watermelon mixture into sterilized jars. Fill within ⅛ inch from top. Wipe rim and threads of jars and cover quickly with lids. Screw threaded bands tightly onto jar, invert jars for 5 minutes, then turn them upright. Leave jars undisturbed until lids seal, about 1 hour.

MAKES 3 PINTS.

Recipe courtesy of Randy Wayne White.

I was up early, as always. Watched the sun push a mesa of gaseous pink light out of eastwardly mangroves. The circumference of the sun was precise, huge, orange as a Nebraska moon. It energized the shallow water of Dinkin's Bay; changed the color from gray to cobalt to purple to tangerine as wading birds glided on an air-foil of their own reflection. The birds ascended, then banked away to feed. —*The Mangrove Coast*, RWW

Seagrape–Key Lime Jelly

The berries of the seagrape tree are red to purple and, like grapes, hang in clusters. The fruit is used in the making of wine and jelly. The trees can reach a height of fifty feet. The leaves are almost round in shape and can be as wide as eight to ten inches in width, turning a magnificent red or golden yellow during the winter months. I like to use the leaves as parchment paper. —RWW

3 quarts ripe purple seagrapes, washed and patted dry

5 tablespoons Key lime juice

5 cups sugar

1 box Certo powdered pectin

Place seagrapes in a large pot. Add water to barely cover. Bring to a boil over medium-high heat and cook until tender. Drain seagrapes and return them to pot. Mash seagrapes and strain through cheesecloth. Measure seagrape juice.

Pour 5 cups juice back into the pot. Add lime juice, sugar, and powdered pectin. Mix well and bring to boil over medium-high heat. Continue boiling, stirring constantly, until jelly sheets from spoon or registers 224°F on a jelly thermometer.

Pour jelly into hot sterilized jars and seal.

MAKES 2 TO 3 DOZEN 8-OUNCE JARS.

Recipe courtesy of Lynda Leonard-Boyce.

Seagrapes

Cranberry Jam

Carlene says this is a family favorite, especially during the Thanksgiving and Christmas holidays. —RWW

2 pounds of frozen cranberries, defrosted

½ pint of water

1½ pounds natural cane sugar

Place cranberries and water in a large saucepan over medium-high heat. Bring mixture to a boil. Reduce heat and simmer until cranberries are soft. Add sugar and bring mixture back to a boil, stirring constantly, until sugar is dissolved and mixture registers 220°F on jelly thermometer. Pour into hot sterilized jars and seal. Process in a boiling-water bath.

MAKES 2 TO 3 DOZEN 8-OUNCE JARS.

Recipe courtesy of Lynda Leonard-Boyce.

Strawberry Freezer Jam

Lynda's homemade jellies and jams at the Sanibel Café were always island favorites, and made popular gifts. —RWW

1 quart strawberries, washed, hulled, and crushed

4 cups sugar

¾ cup water

1 box Sure-Jell fruit pectin

Place crushed strawberries (room temperature) in a large bowl. Add 4 cups sugar and stir to combine. Allow berries to stand for 10 minutes. Mix ¾ cup water and fruit pectin together in a small saucepan. Place over medium-high heat and boil for a minute, stirring constantly. Remove from heat and stir hot pectin mixture into fruit. Continue stirring for 3 minutes.

Ladle into clean, sterilized jars immediately. Cover and seal at once. Allow jars to stand at room temperature for 24 hours. Store jam in freezer. Small amounts may be kept in refrigerator for up to 3 weeks.

MAKES 2 TO 3 DOZEN 8-OUNCE JARS.

Recipe courtesy of Lynda Leonard-Boyce.

Red Raspberry and Peach Jam

This recipe brings back wonderful memories of Sunday breakfast and my mother's hot baked biscuits served with homemade jam. —RWW

    2 cups peeled, pitted, and crushed peaches (about 1½ pounds)

    ¼ cup lemon juice, divided

    2 cups red raspberries

    7 cups sugar

    1 (3-ounce) bottle liquid fruit pectin

    Few drops almond extract

Mix crushed peaches and 2 tablespoons lemon juice together in a large bowl. Allow to rest for 15 minutes. Place raspberries in a medium bowl. Crush berries with the back of a spoon. Add remaining 2 tablespoons lemon juice. Stir to mix.

Place peaches and raspberries in a heavy kettle. Add 7 cups of sugar and stir to mix well. Bring to a full rolling boil over medium-high heat, stirring constantly. Boil 1 minute. Remove from heat and stir in pectin. Skim any foam that has formed. Stir in almond extract and ladle into sterilized half-pint jars to within ⅛ inch from top. Wipe jar rims and secure lids tightly. Process in a boiling-water bath for 5 minutes.

MAKES 4 HALF-PINTS.

Recipe courtesy of Lynda Leonard-Boyce.

Sanibel Causeway

For many, the fascination of water lies in its potential:
the opportunity to converge with elements as basic
as a tidal system, the potential to intersect, in some
precise way, with dynamics that may be intuited but
never fully understood. —*The Best of Outside*, RWW

Algiers Beach on Sanibel Island

CHAPTER 3

APPETIZERS AND SNACKS

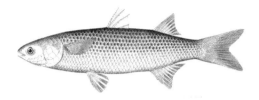

It was a blustery, salt-heavy morning, and I stepped out into a southwest wind that smelled of ocean squalls and waterspouts. —*Tampa Burn,* RWW

A Strange Fish

The black mullet—known around the world as the striped mullet—is a strange-looking creature. It has a blunt, bullet-shaped head and big saucer eyes. It is as aesthetically pleasing as an old Nash Rambler automobile. Because a mullet feeds mostly on detritus and other vegetable matter, it has a gizzardlike stomach that pre-grinds its food before passing it into a freakishly long digestive tract. Earlier in this century [the twentieth], a Florida court once ruled that the mullet, because it had a "gizzard," was actually a bird—thus, freeing a commercial fisherman who was charged with fishing out of season. The incident is but one measure of what a strange fish the mullet is.

—*Captiva,* RWW

Smoked Mullet Dip

Although a strange fish, the meat of the mullet is sweet and succulent. —RWW

2 cups flaked smoked mullet

2 tablespoons mayonnaise

4 tablespoons sour cream

1 pinch Old Bay Seasoning

4 drops Doc Ford's Captiva Sunrise Mojo Rojo (available at www.docford.com)

3 drops Worcestershire sauce

3 drops liquid smoke flavoring (optional)

cracked black pepper

1 lime, cut into wedges

Place mullet, mayonnaise, and sour cream in the bowl of a food processor. Add Old Bay Seasoning, hot sauce, Worcestershire sauce, liquid smoke, and cracked black pepper to taste. Pulse until all ingredients are blended into the consistency of a smooth spread. Adjust seasonings by adding more hot sauce, Worcestershire sauce, and cracked pepper to taste, if desired. Serve with lime wedges, choice of crackers, bread, or chips, and, naturally, a beverage containing alcohol.

MAKES ABOUT 2 CUPS.

Recipe courtesy of Randy Wayne White.

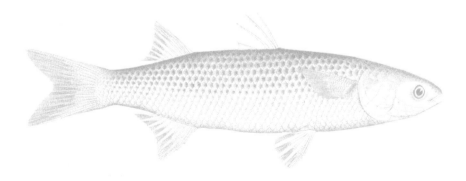

Graeme was always glad to lend a hand.

Shamie Kelly's Hot Crab Dip

Shamie Kelly is Carlene's daughter and an excellent cook. If she hadn't gone to law school, she would have made a superb chef. —RWW

2 (8-ounce) packages Philadelphia Cream Cheese, softened

2 (6-ounce) cans lump crabmeat, drained

3 scallions, chopped

2 tablespoons prepared horseradish

1 tablespoon lemon-pepper seasoning

Preheat oven to 350°F. Place all ingredients in the bowl of an electric mixer. Combine ingredients on low speed until mixture is smooth. Adjust seasonings, adding more horseradish and lemon-pepper seasoning to taste, if desired. Transfer mixture to an ovenproof baking dish that has been coated with vegetable cooking spray and bake, uncovered, for 10 minutes. Stir mixture and return it to oven. Bake 10 minutes more or until mixture is heated through. (Alternately, microwave for 5 minutes; stir; microwave for 3 to 5 more minutes or until heated through.) Serve hot with garlic bagel crisps or crackers.

MAKES ABOUT 3 CUPS.

Recipe courtesy of Shamie Kelly.

Osprey with its catch

"Spread a Little Joy" Hot Cheese Dip

Once a reporter and columnist for the *Sanibel-Captiva Shopper's Guide* in her seventies, Mili Backus interviewed me many times at the marina and attended many functions at Tarpon Bay. Her bubbly personality and positive attitude, not to mention her hot cheese dip, always made her a welcome guest. Mili was Carlene's mother-in-law. —RWW

- 1 (8-ounce) package cream cheese
- 4 ounces prepared French onion dip
- 1½ cups shredded Swiss cheese
- ⅓ cup mayonnaise
- 2 tablespoons chopped onions
- ⅛ teaspoon black pepper
- ⅓ cup pecan and walnut pieces

Preheat oven to 350°F. Place cream cheese, onion dip, Swiss cheese, mayonnaise, onions, and black pepper in a medium bowl. Stirring vigorously with a spoon, combine all ingredients until smooth. Transfer mixture to a deep baking dish that has been coated with vegetable cooking spray. Bake, uncovered, for 8 minutes. Stir mixture and bake for 7 more minutes. Sprinkle nuts atop cheese dip. Serve with assorted crackers and bagel chips.

MAKES ABOUT 2 CUPS.

Recipe courtesy of Terry E. Brennen (Mili's son).

Mili Backus

Cheese Straws

Watching sports at our house as a kid also meant marvelous homemade snacks including Aunt Jewel Wilson McRae's "Can't Eat Just One" Cheese Straws. —RWW

   1 cup sifted all-purpose flour

   ½ teaspoon baking powder

   ¼ teaspoon cayenne pepper

   ½ cup butter (or margarine)

   1 cup shredded cheddar cheese, extra sharp

   3 tablespoons cold water

Sift flour, baking powder and cayenne into bowl. Cut in butter and cheese using a pastry blender, 2 knives or a food processor. Add water and mix well. Fill cookie press (with star tip) and form straws on an ungreased parchment-lined cookie sheet. Make sure to hold cookie press in same horizontal position. Cut into desired lengths. Bake for 9–10 minutes at 375°F. Remove at once. Sprinkle with salt if desired.

MAKES ABOUT 3 DOZEN.

Recipe courtesy of Randy Wayne White.

Jewel Wilson McRae

Teriyaki Wrap-Ups

A simple but tasty appetizer served at our marina parties. —RWW

1 pound sirloin steak

¼ teaspoon powdered ginger

1 tablespoon sugar

½ cup soy sauce

1 tablespoon chopped onions

1 clove garlic, minced

2 (8-ounce) cans whole water chestnuts

Cut sirloin steak into thin strips. Place in a covered container and set aside.

Place ginger, sugar, soy sauce, onions, and garlic in a small bowl. Stir to mix well. Pour marinade over steak strips, cover container, and refrigerate for at least 6 hours.

Preheat broiler. Wrap each steak strip around a water chestnut, securing it with a wooden toothpick. Broil for about 2½ minutes. Turn skewers and broil about 2½ minutes more or until steak is medium-rare. Microwave marinade for 1 minute. Place in a small bowl and serve alongside wrap-ups as a dipping sauce.

MAKES ABOUT 30 WRAP-UPS.

Recipe courtesy of Randy Wayne White.

Twice-Fried Plantains (Tostones)

A staple in many countries. I became very fond of this dish during my travels. —RWW

    2 to 3 green plantains
    7 tablespoons canola oil

Using a sharp knife, cut off the ends of each plantain. Shallowly slice down the sides of each plantain, making four evenly spaced cuts through the skin. Then, starting at the corner of each slit, peel the skin off, until each section is removed.

Cut each plantain crosswise into ½-inch slices.

Place oil in a large skillet and heat over medium-high heat until oil becomes hazy. Working in batches, add as many plantain slices as possible without stacking them. Fry 2 to 3 minutes, turning once, until plantains are browned on both sides.

Remove plantains from oil and place on a brown paper bag to drain. Using a spatula and the heel of your hand, press each plantain into a ¼-inch-thick medallion. Return plantains to skillet and fry for about 1 minute more, turning once. Remove from skillet. Drain on paper towels and serve hot.

MAKES 2 TO 3 DOZEN.

Recipe courtesy of Randy Wayne White.

Deep-Fried Artichoke Hearts with Hot Mustard Sauce

Artichokes are great no matter how you cook them. Deep-fried artichokes with a cold beer can't be beat. —RWW

1 egg

¼ cup white vinegar

¼ cup sugar

¼ cup dry mustard

3 cups canola oil

2 (8-ounce) cans artichoke hearts, drained

Place egg and vinegar in a small bowl. Beat with a wire whisk. Whisk in sugar and dry mustard. Transfer mustard mixture to a small saucepan over medium-high heat. Cook, stirring constantly, until thickened. Remove from heat and set aside to cool to room temperature.

Place a large saucepan over medium-high heat. Add oil and heat to 350°F. Add artichoke hearts and fry until golden brown and leaves begin to open like flowers, about 5 minutes. Drain artichokes on paper toweling. Transfer to a serving dish.

Serve with mustard dipping sauce.

SERVES 6 TO 8.

Recipe courtesy of The Normandie at the West Wind Inn on Sanibel Island.

Sandy Hook Cracked Conch

The Sandy Hook Fish & Rib House is a favorite Pine Island restaurant. It is owned by Richard, Beverly, and Nicole Lauber. Cracked Conch is one of the restaurant's specialties, and is among the best cracked conch I've ever had in my life. —RWW

2 pounds 100 percent cleaned Bahamian conch meat

8 cups oriental bread crumbs

1 tablespoon Old Bay Seasoning

1 tablespoon Greek seasoning (preferably with no MSG)

3 eggs

2 cups milk

1 meat tenderizer or puncture-type mallet

2 cups flour

canola oil or olive oil

First, 100 percent cleaned conch is the best to get. If all you can find is 85 percent, it will work. You will just have to get approximately 3 pounds and will have to do a lot more work to clean it.

Mix the oriental bread crumbs, Old Bay, and Greek seasoning together. In a separate bowl, whip eggs and milk together. This is the egg wash. Take your conch meat and beat it for about 1 minute, or until your hand goes numb and your arm wants to fall off! (This can be a two-beer job.—RWW) Make it as tender as possible, since conch is a relatively tough muscle. Dip conch meat in the egg wash and then coat with flour. Dip into the egg wash, and then lay conch in bread crumb mixture and cover on both sides. Press to make sure crumbs adhere to conch. Next, fry conch in oil heated to 350°F for about 1 minute or until a light, golden brown. Don't wait until it looks dark brown; if you do, it will become like leather you could attach to your shoes. You could also sauté it in olive oil until it becomes light, golden brown if you prefer. You can eat it as is, or serve it with a spicy mayo mixture like we do at Sandy Hook.

SERVES 4.

Recipe courtesy of the Sandy Hook Fish & Rib House in Matlacha, Florida.

Captain Beard's Addictive Guacamole

This recipe comes direct from Captain Scott Beard, dockmaster of the Useppa Island Yacht Club and a frequent surfer on the Costa Rican coast. This dish is best served with tortilla chips, lemon slices, and ice-cold Imperial beer. —RWW

- 2 large Florida avocados or 6 California avocados, pitted, peeled, and diced
- ½ cup finely chopped Vidalia onions
- ¼ cup finely chopped red bell pepper
- ¼ cup finely chopped cubanelle pepper juice from 2 lemons
- 2 tablespoons Tiger Sauce
- ½ teaspoon red Tabasco Sauce
- ½ teaspoon Doc Ford's Tomlinson's Columbian Gold Hot Sauce (available at www.docford.com)
- 3 tablespoons Lizano Salsa Sauce (available at www.amazon.com)
- 3 dashes lemon-pepper seasoning
- 1 tablespoon mayonnaise
- 3 tablespoons sour cream
- ½ teaspoon cumin

Place all ingredients in a large mixing bowl. Gently stir to combine all ingredients. (Texture of the mixture should be somewhat chunky, not creamy.) Refrigerate for 1 hour before serving. Serve with tortilla chips.

MAKES ABOUT 2 CUPS.

Recipe courtesy of Captain Scott Beard.

White pelicans at Tarpon Bay

My charter boat at Tarpon Bay Marina

CHAPTER 4

SOUPS, STEWS, CHOWDERS, GAZPACHO, AND CHILI

Normally, I enjoy running a boat at night. I like being out there alone in the darkness, suspended above the water, going fast. Like gauging my progress by the shapes of the islands, by the positions of distant lights. Like the way the wind washes past, a force so steady that, at times, it seems as if my boat is being held motionless by a jet stream of black air. —*Captiva*, RWW

Belizean Chicken Stew

Belize City is a rat hole but the country people are wonderful and great cooks.—RWW

3 tablespoons canola oil

2 to 3 pounds chicken, cut in pieces

2 quarts water

2 cloves garlic, minced

salt and pepper

3 whole cloves

2 teaspoons oregano

¼ cup vinegar

2 to 3 whole jalapeño or Serrano chile peppers (optional)

1 pound onions

Place oil in a large soup pot over medium-high heat. When oil is hot, add chicken and sauté, turning frequently, until it is browned. Add 2 quarts water, garlic, salt and pepper to taste, cloves, oregano, vinegar, and chile peppers. Bring water to boil, then reduce heat to medium-low and cook until chicken is tender, about 20 to 30 minutes.

Meanwhile, peel onions and cut them into rings. Place onions in a large bowl and add warm water to cover. Allow onions to soak for 30 minutes. Drain onions and add them to soup pot. Cook 20 minutes. Serve with tortillas.

SERVES 4 TO 6.

Recipe courtesy of Randy Wayne White.

Captain Neville Robeson (right) with tarpon charter at Tarpon Bay Marina

"B" Brothers Chili

Shopping at Bailey's General Store on Sanibel is always a little like coming home—even your first time. —RWW

1 tablespoon olive oil

1 large onion, peeled and chopped

1 green bell pepper, seeded and chopped

1 pound ground beef

1 (1-pound, 13-ounce) can tomatoes

1½ teaspoons salt

¼ teaspoon paprika

⅛ teaspoon red pepper flakes

5 whole cloves

3 bay leaves

2 teaspoons chili powder

1 (20-ounce) can red kidney beans, drained

Place a large soup pot over medium heat. Add olive oil. When oil is hot, add onion, bell pepper, and ground beef. Sauté until meat is browned and onions are translucent. Drain off excess fat. Add tomatoes with juice, salt, paprika, red pepper flakes, cloves, bay leaves, and chili powder. Stir well to combine. Reduce heat to low, cover pot, and simmer for 2 hours. Add drained beans and heat thoroughly.

SERVES 4 TO 6.

Recipe courtesy of Francis and Sam Bailey of Bailey's General Store on Sanibel Island.

Broccoli Soup

Nothing tasted better on a cold winter night than a bowl of my Aunt JoAnn Wilson Byers' steaming hot broccoli soup and a basket of my grandmother Nayrilla's piping hot corn bread (see page 15). It is inspiring knowing that I come from a family of cooks. —RWW

1 cup onion, chopped

4 tablespoons butter

3 tablespoons flour

½ teaspoon garlic powder

6 cups water

6 chicken bouillon cubes

1 (8 ounce) package thin/fine egg noodles

1 teaspoon salt

1 teaspoon pepper

2 (10–ounce) packages chopped broccoli, frozen

6 cups milk

1 pound Velveeta cheese, cubed

JoAnn Wilson Byers

Sauté onions in 4 tablespoons of butter for three minutes. Add flour and cook for two minutes. Sprinkle in ½ teaspoon garlic powder. Add 6 cups of water and 6 bouillon cubes. Whisk and bring to a boil. Gradually add egg noodles and 1 teaspoon of salt and 1 teaspoon of pepper. Cook noodles until done. Stir in 2 boxes of broccoli. Add 6 cups of milk and 1 pound of cubed Velveeta cheese once broccoli is tender. Stir until cheese is melted, being careful not to break up noodles. JoAnn sometimes used a fork to check the bottom of the pot instead of a spoon.

MAKES 8 SERVINGS.

Recipe courtesy of Randy Wayne White.

Calamity Jane's Gazpacho

Gazpacho was a lunchtime favorite at Calamity Jane's on Sanibel. Carlene's crew from the *Sanibel-Captiva Shopper's Guide* spent many lunch breaks at this cozy café. Although the restaurant has changed hands several times the marvelous meals served by Jane and her staff will never be forgotten. —RWW

2 (10-ounce) cans peeled tomatoes, minced

4 ripe tomatoes, peeled and minced

1 large cucumber, peeled, seeded, and minced

2 large green bell peppers, cored, seeded, and minced

1 large red onion, peeled and minced

¼ cup olive oil

¼ cup red wine vinegar

1 large clove garlic, minced

2 tablespoons finely chopped fresh basil

1 teaspoon cumin

1 tablespoon minced fresh cilantro

1 teaspoon black pepper

1 tablespoon minced fresh parsley

1 teaspoon dried thyme

½ teaspoon red pepper flakes (optional)

Mix all ingredients together in a large glass or plastic bowl. Cover with cling wrap and refrigerate to chill. Jane never used a blender or food processor but finely minced the vegetables by hand. She always said that if you use a blender or food processor, do not over process.

SERVES 6 TO 8.

Captain Neville Robeson aboard his boat *Copenhagen*

The breeze blowing off the water was suddenly chilly
. . . sweet with ozone and electricity. —*Gone*, RWW

Chicken in Coconut Soup (Tom Kha Gai)

A popular dish at the Bangkok House on Sanibel. A memory from the past. —RWW

1 cup sliced, boneless chicken breast

1 tablespoon sliced galangal ("kha" available at Asian grocery stores)

2 cans coconut milk

2 tablespoons fish sauce

2 tablespoons fresh lemon or lime juice

1 tablespoon chili powder

1 tablespoon chopped fresh cilantro

Place chicken, galangal, and coconut milk in a large saucepan over medium heat. Cook, stirring occasionally, until chicken is tender. Remove saucepan from heat. Add fish sauce and lemon or lime juice. Stir to combine ingredients. Transfer to a serving dish. Sprinkle with chili powder and cilantro. Serve immediately.

SERVES 6.

For me, fishing had more to do with the cleaning table than with ceremony. It was interlude to work, then it became work. I hung corpses out to dry; I stacked them in coolers. Fishing was a means, not an end. What I liked about it was being on the water, but you don't have to have a rod in your hand to be on the water. —*The Best of Outside*, RWW

Conch Chowder

There are many variations of conch chowder. This recipe is a favorite of Carlene's. —RWW

- 1 pound conch meat
- 2 large carrots
- 1 large red onion
- 4 stalks celery
- 1 (14½-ounce) can Del Monte Italian stewed tomatoes
- 1 large (16-ounce) can V8 juice
- ¼ cup Worcestershire sauce
- 1 teaspoon dried basil
- 1 teaspoon dried thyme
- 1 teaspoon Doc Ford's Green Flash Hot Sauce (available at www.docford.com)
- 2 large potatoes, diced

In food processor, using steel blade, chop the conch, carrots, onion, and celery very finely in batches. Add tomatoes and V8 juice and all the seasonings. Simmer for 1 hour, then add the potatoes and continue cooking until the potatoes are tender. Serve with hard, crusty bread.

MAKES ABOUT 2 QUARTS.

Recipe courtesy of Carlene Fredericka Brennen.

Guatemalan Juliana Soup

A simple but tasty meal. Great after a day of hunting fish. During a Revolution in the late 1980s, I drove all over Guatemala in a pickup truck. Guys with guns showed me this one. —RWW

2 tablespoons olive oil

1 cleaned leek, or 1 peeled medium onion, chopped

pepper

ground turmeric

1 turnip, peeled and chopped

4 medium carrots, peeled and chopped

2 small zucchini or yellow squash, chopped

¼ head cabbage, chopped

1 cup corn

3 potatoes, peeled and chopped

1 cup cooked, diced chicken

1 quart chicken broth or 2 bouillon cubes and 1 quart water

salt

Place a large soup pot over medium heat. Add olive oil. When oil is hot, add chopped leek or onion, a dash of pepper, and a pinch of ground turmeric. Sauté leeks until translucent. Add chopped turnip, carrots, squash, cabbage, corn, and potatoes. Also add diced chicken. Add chicken broth to soup pot and raise heat to high. When mixture comes to a boil, reduce heat to medium-low and simmer until vegetables are tender. Season with salt to taste.

SERVES 4 TO 6.

Recipe courtesy of Randy Wayne White.

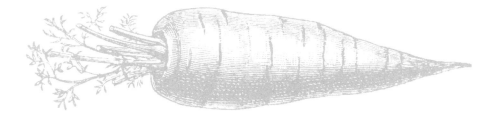

Sanibel Island Chili

The Sanibel Island Cuervo Gold Chili team—Terri Blackmore, Dan Toolan, Bob Swinker, Shamie Kelly, and Carlene Fredericka Brennen—won an award at the Suncoast District Chili Cook-Off competition at the Dunes on Sanibel for two years running with this recipe. Good friends all, the team shares a love for chili and for Cuervo Gold. For qualification purposes, this prize-winning recipe makes a whopping 3 gallons of chili. —RWW

12 tablespoons (1½ sticks) butter, divided

2 pounds chuck steak, cubed

4 to 5 pounds ground beef (chuck steak)

3½ pounds ground pork

salt and pepper

3 large onions, diced

4 green bell peppers, seeded and diced

4 to 5 cloves garlic, minced

1 jar mild banana peppers, chopped, juice reserved

1 (12-ounce) can beer

1 small jalapeño pepper, seeded and chopped

6 large tomatoes, coarsely chopped

1 (16-ounce) can tomato puree

½ cup chili powder (or more to taste)

¼ cup cumin (more to taste if needed)

8 to 10 dashes ground cloves

1 teaspoon cayenne pepper

¾ cup picante sauce

3½ tablespoons brown sugar

½ square Baker's dark chocolate

¼ to ½ cup Jose Cuervo Gold Tequila

Place 6 tablespoons of butter in a large soup pot over medium-high heat. (Pot must be large enough to accommodate 10 to 12 pounds of meat). When butter has melted, add cubed chuck steak. Sauté chuck, stirring frequently, until browned. Slowly add ground beef and ground pork and sauté, stirring frequently, until browned. Transfer meat to a colander to drain off excess fat. Discard any fat left in pot. Off-burner, return meat to pot. Season meat with salt and pepper to taste.

Meanwhile, place 6 tablespoons of butter in another large pot over medium heat. When butter has melted, add onions, bell peppers, minced garlic, and chopped banana peppers and sauté, stirring frequently, until onions are translucent.

Place meat pot over medium heat. Transfer onion mixture to meat pot. Stir to combine ingredients. Add beer, chopped jalapeño pepper, and reserved banana pepper juice. Stir well to combine. Add chopped tomatoes, tomato puree, chili powder, cumin, cloves, and cayenne pepper. Stir to combine ingredients.

Cover pot, reduce heat to low, and simmer, stirring occasionally, for 1½ to 2 hours. (For thicker chili, only partially cover pot with lid.) After 1 hour, adjust salt, cayenne pepper, chili powder, and cumin to taste. Thirty minutes before turning off the burner, add picante sauce and brown sugar. Add the chocolate and tequila 15 minutes before serving.

SERVES A CROWD.

Recipe courtesy of the Cuervo Gold Chili Team.

Dan Toolan, Terri Blackmore, and Shamie Kelly

Scallop Stew

I love snorkeling the shallow-water grass flats, gathering live scallops. The bays of Southwest Florida produce the sweetest specimens in my experience, and this recipe is an ideal way to enjoy them. —RWW

¼ cup butter, divided

1 quart scallops

1 tablespoon flour

1 quart milk, scalded

1 teaspoon salt

⅛ teaspoon pepper

1 teaspoon paprika

Place 2 tablespoons of the butter in a medium skillet over medium heat. When butter has melted, add scallops and sauté for 5 minutes.

Meanwhile, fill lower portion of a large double boiler halfway full. Place over medium heat and bring to a boil. Place remaining butter in top portion of double boiler. When butter has melted, add flour and stir to form a roux. Slowly stir in scalded milk. Reduce heat to low. Add salt and pepper and stir constantly until sauce has thickened, about 5 minutes.

Add scallops and stir until scallops are heated through. Divide among individual serving bowls and sprinkle with paprika.

SERVES 4.

Recipe courtesy of Lynda Leonard-Boyce.

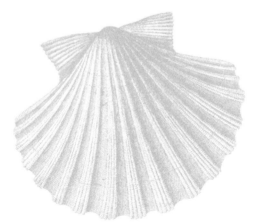

Sue Gray's Sanibel Soup

Sue's soup was popular at island gatherings and it's a staple at Carlene's house. It was also a favorite at the local firehouse. —RWW

1 pound ground beef or turkey

1 (14-ounce) can corn

1 (15-ounce) can kidney beans

1 (15-ounce) can black beans

1 (15-ounce) can pinto beans

1 (10-ounce) can Rotel tomatoes with green chilies

1 (14½-ounce) can Mexican stewed tomatoes

1 (1-ounce) package Hidden Valley Ranch Dressing

1 (1½-ounce) package McCormick Taco Seasoning

Place beef or turkey in a large soup pot over medium heat. Brown meat, stirring occasionally. Drain excess fat. Add corn, beans, tomatoes, and seasonings. Stir to combine ingredients. Bring mixture to a boil. Reduce heat to low and simmer for 20 minutes. Serve with hard-crusted bread.

SERVES 6.

Recipe courtesy of Carlene Fredericka Brennen, in memory of her dear friend Sue Gray.

Sanibel Island sunset

Yellow-Tomato Gazpacho with Medallions of Florida Lobster

Captain Matt Mitchell is a talented chef. This is one of his most popular recipes.—RWW

6 large ripe yellow tomatoes, cored, seeded, and roughly chopped

1 sweet yellow bell pepper, cored, seeded, and roughly chopped

1 English cucumber, peeled and cut into 1-inch chunks

1 small sweet onion, roughly chopped

2 tablespoons olive oil

1 tablespoon rice wine vinegar

salt and white pepper

2 Florida lobster tails

Place tomatoes, bell pepper, cucumber, onion, olive oil, and vinegar in a blender and process until smooth. Using the back of a wooden spoon, push mixture through a fine strainer. Season with salt and pepper to taste. Place in a covered container and refrigerate to chill at least 2 hours, to marry flavors.

Place a large pot of salted water over medium-high heat and bring it to a boil. Drop lobster tails in water and boil until shells turn red, about 10 minutes. Remove lobster from shells and slice into medallions. Place medallions in a covered container and refrigerate to chill for 1 hour.

To serve, ladle gazpacho into shallow soup bowls. Divide lobster medallions equally among servings and place them atop the soup.

SERVES 4 TO 6.

Recipe courtesy of Captain Matt Mitchell, St. James City, Florida.

Cabbage Palms in the Bailey Tract of the
J. N. "Ding" Darling National Wildlife Refuge

CHAPTER 5

SALADS

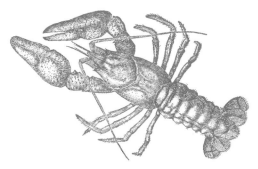

Stepping out into the summer night was like stepping into warm water, but with sounds and odors. Fragrance of night flowers. Thunk-whap of jumping mullet. Sulfuric gas oozing from the mangrove muck like a long hot breath.

—*The Heat Islands*, RWW

Hearts of Palm Salad with Creole Grilled Grouper

This is another wonderful dish courtesy of Captain Matt Mitchell. —RWW

Citrus Vinaigrette:

juice of 6 oranges

1 shallot, peeled and sliced

¼ cup rice wine vinegar

1 tablespoon Dijon mustard

¼ cup cilantro leaves

½ cup canola oil

salt and pepper

Salad:

1 quart of water

1 pound fresh hearts of palm

4 heads frisée

2 heads Boston bib lettuce

1 head radicchio

1 pint yellow grape tomatoes

Grouper Fillets:

¼ cup blackening seasoning

2 tablespoons olive oil

6 (6-ounce) grouper fillets

I taught Carlene to fly fish.

For the vinaigrette: Place orange juice, shallot, vinegar, mustard, and cilantro leaves in a small bowl. Whisk in canola oil and salt and pepper to taste. Place in a covered container and refrigerate until needed.

For the salad: Place 1 quart water in a large saucepan over medium-high heat. Add hearts of palm and cook until tender. Drain hearts of palm; refresh with cold water; drain again. Slice hearts of palm on a 45° angle. Place hearts in a medium glass or plastic container. Pour citrus vinaigrette over hearts. Cover, refrigerate, and allow hearts to marinate for 2 hours.

Raccoons are amazing creatures.

Wash frisée, bib, and radicchio and spin-dry. Tear into bite-size pieces. Divide greens among 6 dinner plates. Drain hearts of palm and reserve citrus vinaigrette. Place hearts and grape tomatoes atop greens.

For the grouper fillets: Preheat grill. Mix blackening seasoning and olive oil in a medium bowl. Dredge grouper fillets in seasoning. Grill fillets 10 minutes per inch of thickness or until fish flakes when tested with a fork.

Place 1 grouper fillet atop greens on each dinner plate. Drizzle fish and greens with citrus vinaigrette.

SERVES 6.

Recipe courtesy of Captain Matt Mitchell, St. James City, Florida.

Seafood Pasta Salad

Gramma Dot's Seaside Saloon is located at Sanibel Marina. Carlene tournament-tarpon-fished aboard her boat *Tarpon Times* out of this marina for many years. After the tournaments, the club members and charter guides would congregate at the restaurant's comfortable oak bar, enjoying lots of cold beer and reliving the highlights of the day. The seafood pasta salad was always a favorite after a day of fishing; topped off with more cold beer, it made for a perfect day. —RWW

¾ pound angel hair or linguine

1 large onion, chopped

½ stalk celery, diced

1½ pounds each of cooked shrimp, lobster, and scallops

2 cups mayonnaise

1 cup sour cream

¼ cup fresh tarragon chopped

1 teaspoon seasoned salt

¾ cup grated Parmesan cheese

cherry tomatoes

Break pasta into ¾-inch lengths. Fill a large pot with water and place over medium-high heat. When water comes to a boil, add pasta and cook al dente following package instructions. Drain pasta.

Place pasta, onion, celery, seafood, mayonnaise, and sour cream in a large bowl. Stir to combine ingredients. Add tarragon and seasoned salt. Toss to mix well. Add Parmesan cheese and toss again. Cover and refrigerate until chilled. Serve garnished with cherry tomatoes.

SERVES 8.

Recipe courtesy of Gramma Dot's Seaside Saloon at Sanibel Marina on Sanibel Island.

Bottlenose dolphin and manatee can be seen frequently in Tarpon Bay, delighting visitors.

Sliced Tomato Genovese

A delightful dish from The Jacaranda. Restaurant manager Patrick Harder has hosted some marvelous book signings for me in the lovely garden patio of this Sanibel Island restaurant. — RWW

¼ cup balsamic vinegar

⅔ cup plus 1 tablespoon olive oil

3 tablespoons chopped fresh basil

1 large ripe tomato, cut into four slices

2 ounces grated Parmesan cheese

¼ cup fresh bread crumbs

1 teaspoon chopped garlic

2 slices whole-milk mozzarella cheese

2 slices red onion

salt and pepper

Place vinegar, ⅔ cup olive oil, and chopped basil in a small bowl. Whisk to mix well. Set vinaigrette aside.

Place 2 tomato slices on each of 2 plates so that they overlap slightly. Place Parmesan cheese, bread crumbs, 1 tablespoon olive oil, and garlic in a small bowl and stir to mix. Sprinkle the mixture evenly atop the tomato slices. Top tomatoes on each plate with 1 slice mozzarella and 1 slice red onion. Drizzle salad with basil vinaigrette. Season with salt and pepper to taste.

SERVES 2.

Recipe courtesy of The Jacaranda on Sanibel Island.

Tarpon Bay Crab Salad

We used to eat this wonderful salad between charters. Served chilled, it's great on a hot day. I've added my hot sauce to the recipe to spice the salad up a notch. —RWW

1 pound blue-crab meat

1 green bell pepper, diced

1 onion, diced

2 ribs celery, diced

⅓ cup prepared cocktail sauce

⅔ cup mayonnaise

Tomlinson's Colombian Gold Hot Sauce (available at www.docford.com) to taste

1 teaspoon dill weed

salt and pepper

Place crabmeat, bell pepper, onion, and celery in a large bowl. Toss to mix well. Add cocktail sauce, mayonnaise, hot sauce, and dill weed, and toss to mix until all ingredients are well coated. Season with salt and pepper to taste.

SERVES 4.

Recipe courtesy of Randy Wayne White.

A snowy egret enjoys a plump shrimp.

CHAPTER 6

CEVICHE

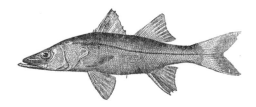

Ecosystems take thousands of years to balance interlinkings between geography and species. The resulting milieu is not a stage for experimentation. Tinkering is a recipe for disaster that's been demonstrated too many times. —*Dead of Night*, RWW

In Search of the Finest Ceviche

It was Paloma Magallanes, a spirited but untraveled grandmother, who unwittingly convinced me to spend a week in a tiny seaside village in Baja, Mexico, that I'd never heard of and certainly never planned to visit. I stayed only because the woman possessed a great gift that cast an ungodly spell on me. Fellow Third World sojourners will appreciate the reason: good food and lots of it.

Paloma is waitress, head cook, and owner of the tiny Restaurante El Faro in Puerto Adolfo Lopez Mateos, a town of dusty streets, sleepy chickens, and wandering dogs on Baja's Pacific coast. El Faro is a pleasant open-air bistro with a dirt courtyard and six Formica-topped tables. There's a plywood ceiling and a bright seascape hand painted on the front window. Off to one side, Paloma has arranged four old mismatched recliners, to facilitate digestion.

Even with its few tables, El Faro's seating capacity seems optimistic when you consider the fact that the village of Puerto Adolfo Lopez Mateos has fewer than a hundred souls and isn't even shown on most maps. In a country weary of injustice,

Mexico's geographers perhaps decided it was unfair that a settlement so small should have a name that took up so much space and required so much labor.

To find Puerto Adolfo Lopez Mateos (whose name locals have efficiently shortened to "Lopez Mateos"), follow the Pacific coast of Baja south about three-fourths of the way down until the barrier island of Isla Magdalena swoops dramatically westward. The land shift is so abrupt that it's as if, in some long-gone geological epic, the island attempted to sneak away from its desert host but failed. Look inland and you'll see an estuary—Bahia Magdalena, or Mag Bay, as it's known to gringos. Lopez Mateos is to the north, where the barrier island squeezes close to the mainland. If you arrive by boat, you'll see the bare dunes of Isla Magdalena and then a large factory of blue and beige corrugated metal. The complex is fenced, and there are guards at the gate. This is the Mareden fish cannery, the village's only employer and one of two sources of income—the other being the tourists who come each spring to watch the annual migration of gray whales through Magdalena Bay. Lopez Mateos is, in short, a company town. Every morning, a steam whistle awakens the citizenry at six and calls employees to work, from ten till seven. Ten hours later, the whistle sends the workers home again.

Late one morning my friend Galen Hanselman and I were walking east past the cannery, heading toward the white church at the center of town, when we stumbled into Paloma's restaurant. We'd been flying all over Baja in Galen's Cessna 182, and we'd originally planned to make a pit stop here in Lopez Mateos—thinking, instead that we'd spend the night a little further south along the bay, in a place called San Carlos (an uninteresting tourist town, it turned out). But our plan began to cave in as soon as we sat at one of the little Formica tables. We could have sat anywhere—we were the only living creatures in the place except for a dog lying beside one of the chairs. Eventually, a chunky Mexican woman approached. She had a flat, handsome face with vaguely Gaelic features, and she walked with the swagger of a trail hand.

Had we come for a meal?

Yes, we told her, a light lunch perhaps. She nodded with the kind of approval that one associates with grandmothers who like to see people eat. We expected her to return with menus. Instead, she returned wiping ice from three bottles of Pacifico Clara beer and carrying a very large ceramic bowl. One of the bottles was for herself. She toasted: "To the good life!"

In a bowl was ceviche: chunks of raw fish, onions, varieties of peppers and tomatoes, all soaked in lime juice. Ceviche, made properly and served fresh, is one of the great concoctions of the world, the bouillabaisse of the tropics. But even in the best restaurants ceviche is usually a disappointment, if not downright dangerous.

Galen dipped a spoon into the bowl and tasted experimentally. He looked at me and dipped the spoon again.

With my charter's tarpon catch

"Hey!" he said. He began to scoop the ceviche onto his plate. "You're not going to believe this stuff," he said. "It's really good."

No, it was great. Maybe the best ceviche I'd ever had. Next Paloma brought salad, tortillas, and a bowl of frijoles. "My God," Galen said. "These beans! Have you tried the beans?"

Keep in mind that we'd been flying all over Baja, a great peninsula in a great nation where people really know how to make beans. But truly, Paloma's beans were the beans of an artist.

Then she brought out a platter of grilled fish. It was corvine, a genus common in coastal Mexico and closely related to the weakfish of the Atlantic seaboard. It's a nice fish to eat, very mild tasting, but not particularly firm. Yet somehow Paloma's artistry transcended the frailties of the species.

Galen and I sat there feasting, and Paloma kept bringing food. We hadn't ordered; there were no menus. But we'd come for a meal, and that's what the woman was serving us. As we ate, she'd sometimes swing into a chair at our table and talk. Had we come in the small plane that recently landed? Yes, we'd come in the small plane, a fact that seemed to either interest her or impress her, I couldn't tell which.

Did we like the food? Yes, we loved the food, which made her grin. We were very lucky to have the fish, she said. It was the last she had. "I buy only fresh fish!" she said. "The fishermen know that I'm very fussy!"

As we ate dessert (papaya with lime juice and sliced wild oranges), I noticed Galen glancing at his watch. "I guess we have to get going, huh?" I said.

"Yeah, I guess so," he said. He was drumming his fingers on the table. "But, my God, that was really some meal."

"The best."

"Extraordinary."

"Really extraordinary."

I wondered if Galen was contemplating the same thing I was. "When you think about it," I said, "discovering great food on the road, food this good, is a rare thing indeed." He was nodding his head. "Can you imagine what it would be like to eat dinner here?"

You bet I could imagine it. Dinner, breakfast, too, and maybe lunch again. The only problem was, Paloma really was out of fish.

No problem. On Hanselman's plane I had stowed a fifteen-horsepower Mercury outboard motor and a beautiful little Avon inflatable boat. And as I've already explained, the village of Puerto Adolfo Lopez Mateos is on Magdalena Bay, a place teeming with fish.

Bahia Magdalena is formed by a 130-mile-long string of sand barrier islands that are separated by deepwater cuts or passes (*bocas,* they are called), which allow ingress from the Pacific and which have made the bay a favorite harbor on this isolated coast. Its history is not unlike the history of all wild anchorages that are rich in resources except for one: freshwater. Although indigenous people lived here off and on since before the time of Christ, they were necessarily migratory. In the late 1800s, a US land company settled five thousand Americans on the bay, but the colony failed. It wasn't until the late 1930s, when deep wells were sunk, that the region slowly began to acquire a permanent populace.

Mag Bay's backwater littoral remains pristine, wind cropped, wild with light, and seldom traveled. There's a good reason for this: It's extremely shallow, sometimes just a couple of feet deep, a fact that poses serious access problems and makes it a perfect place for sea kayaks and fast little inflatables like the Avon.

I tried to explain all this to Galen; the man is brilliant when it comes to aviation, but he's from Idaho, for God's sake, and knows nothing about the sea. I told him, "Visit any of the remote estuaries in the world, and the problem is always access. It's frustrating. All the fish you could ever want to catch, great birding and exploring, but you can't get on the water. This little Avon changed all that. We can go anyplace."

Galen was dubious. All week long, the wind had blown a steady twenty knots, but on this cloudy afternoon had freshened to twenty-five. The bay had a menacing arctic glow about it. Still, we were headed for the mangroves estuaries, not the open sea. And we were prepared.

We'd packed several gallons of water, flashlights, military-issue MREs, and paddles. Besides, we were on a mission: The Restaurante El Faro needed fish. We weren't just fishermen; we were providers. True, we mostly wanted to provide for ourselves, but the mandate was compelling even if the intent was selfish. Anglers and travelers must be allowed our small dishonesties.

I indulged in a second dishonesty. I'd read here and there that one of my favorite gamefish, the snook, also known as robalo, could possibly be caught in Magdalena Bay. None of the writers, however, claimed to have caught one, nor did they claim to know anyone who had. Indeed, the tone of the articles treated the snook like a shadowy creature of Baja legend. Well, I, for one, wanted to prove that the snook could indeed be caught in Mag Bay.

That afternoon we headed out in the Avon, crashing through waves. We went north along the mainland shore until I found a mangrove point where there was an interesting confluence of tidal rips. It looked like a great place to fish.

My first cast—boom. I played and landed a big corvine. Second cast—boom. I played and landed a California halibut that had to weigh ten pounds. A few casts later, I got a nice sea bass.

Galen didn't try to hide his surprise. "You actually caught something!" He hustled toward the boat to get his rod.

Back in the village, Galen and I drew a crowd as we walked through the streets shouldering the weight of a stringer full of fish. In the evening, lounging in one of the big mismatched recliners after one of the finest dinners I've ever had, I said to Galen, "You know, we can leave tomorrow, but I'd bet anything there are snook on that point. I'd hate to fly out without proving it." I proceeded to give him a detailed explanation of tides and habitat to prove that my claim had merit.

He not only accepted this fiction—he embraced it. "Snook, damn right," he said. "They've got to be there. We should stay."

We did. For several days. We ate, we fished, we slept, and then we fished some more—though we never saw a single snook. In the evenings, Galen and I would roam the streets, listening to music emanating from the white church, conversing with the local fishermen at the docks. They claimed they often caught robalo. We never saw one among the piles of fish they did catch, but they were good stories to hear as we stood among the mud and small boats, drinking beer with them.

We'd rented a cheap room at a boardinghouse, but the restaurant was our real home. We stopped there three or four times a day. At each meal, Paloma,

Fishing Pine Island Sound

brilliant Paloma, who had achieved an expanded artistry in this small, small place, swaggered about, bringing us more of this, more of that. She spent more and more time sitting at our table, asking us about places we'd been, places we were going, and she seemed particularly interested in Galen's Cessna. "Many men in this village would be afraid to leave the ground in a plane," she boasted. "But not me! I would never be afraid!"

It finally dawned on us. "She wants to go for a ride," Galen said.

So on our last morning in Puerto Adolfo Lopez Mateos, we escorted Paloma Magallanes of the Restaurante El Faro through dusty streets to the landing strip. It was early. The steam whistle had just called villagers to work at the Mareden cannery, but Paloma ignored their stares with regal indifference.

It was no wonder that they stared. Despite the intense morning heat, Paloma wore a long dress, a cape, jewelry, makeup, and a furry hat that came down over her ears. Also, the sand apparently made it difficult to walk in high heels.

When I told her that she looked as if she was going to a party, this normally talkative woman didn't reply. Indeed, she said nothing until we were banking over the emptiness of Magdalena Bay. It was then that she finally braved her first peek out the window, touched her face with trembling fingers, and smiled.

There was no swagger in her smile, only a trace of wistfulness. For the first time, she looked down on the little swatch of bleached sand and turquoise sea that had defined her entire life. "It's something I always wanted to do," she said. "I always wanted to know what it feels like, just once to fly away."

—*Last Flight Out*, RWW

Ceviche de Hotel Hemingway

Some of the best ceviche I ever tasted was found in the restaurants of the small Havana hotels where I stayed during my travels through Cuba. —RWW

1 pound mild-flavored, deboned raw fish fillets, cut into ½-inch chunks

½ onion, finely chopped

½ red or green bell pepper, cored, seeded, and finely chopped

3 sprigs fresh cilantro, finely chopped

juice of 5 to 6 limes

Place fish, onion, bell pepper, and cilantro in a medium glass bowl. Add lime juice and stir gently, so that all ingredients are fully submerged in the juice. Cover with cling wrap and refrigerate for 2 hours to allow fish to cook in the lime juice. Serve ceviche on soda crackers. (Some Costa Ricans add ketchup and mayonnaise to the ceviche before serving.)

MAKES ABOUT 2 CUPS.

Recipe courtesy of Randy Wayne White.

Sanibel Island Lighthouse

Conch Salad

This is one of Carlene's favorite dishes, served at The Lazy Flamingo on Periwinkle Way. This eatery was once the headquarters for the Tropical Twins Fan Club. Avid baseball fans Carlene and her friend Terri Blackmore were co-presidents of the club and were once asked to throw out balls at a Red Sox–Minnesota Twins spring training game in Fort Myers.—RWW

1½ pounds queen conch, cleaned, pounded, and diced

1 onion, diced

2 green bell peppers, cored, seeded, and diced

1 red bell pepper, cored, seeded, and diced

3 tomatoes, seeded and diced

1 cup fresh lime juice

1 cup water

salt and pepper

2 limes, cut into wedges

Place conch, onion, bell peppers, and tomatoes in a large glass bowl. Add lime juice and water and stir to mix. Add salt and pepper to taste. Cover bowl with cling wrap and refrigerate for at least 30 minutes to allow conch to cook in the lime juice.

Serve with crackers and a thick lime wedge.

MAKES ABOUT 2 CUPS.

Recipe courtesy of The Lazy Flamingo (at two locations) on Sanibel Island.

White Ibis at Bowman's Beach

Shrimp Ceviche

At Tarpon Bay Marina, the fresh live shrimp we didn't use as bait we used as appetizers.—RWW

1½ pounds fresh raw Florida pink shrimp, peeled and deveined

2 cups Key lime juice

½ cup finely chopped green bell pepper

½ cup white wine

1 cup finely chopped onion

3 medium tomatoes, seeded and chopped

½ cup finely chopped cilantro

3 drops Tomlinson's Columbian Gold Hot Sauce (available at www.docford.com)

salt and pepper

Place shrimp, Key lime juice, bell pepper, white wine, onion, tomatoes, cilantro, and hot sauce in a large glass mixing bowl. Toss to mix well. Season with salt and pepper to taste. Cover bowl with cling wrap and refrigerate for 2 to 3 hours so that shrimp can cook in the lime juice.

SERVES 4 TO 6.

Recipe courtesy of Randy Wayne White.

Just being alone in a fast boat improved my mind, feeling sunlight and smelling the wind. —*Gone*, RWW

How Dead Bern's Ceviche Got Its Name

My friend Bayardo ran a cattle ranch on the Pacific Coast of Costa Rica. I think he called because he felt my last visit there was not a successful one, what with the broken generator, the dead cook, and the peasant woman who ran screaming into the night.

"This time it will be better," he told me on the telephone. Like so many Costa Ricans, he tended to blame himself for any small thing that goes very wrong.

Slightly more than a year before, I had been sitting on the porch of his ranch house, reading by lantern light (the generator was out), which I enjoyed. The lantern attracted moths and bats more surely than electric bulbs, and it was pleasant to sit with jungle on all sides and watch animals flutter in and out of the darkness. But then I heard a scream that was not pleasant—a primal wail that brought me to my feet, heart pounding. I ran along the porch toward the back of the house to find Bayardo and several of his workers trying to comfort a maid who was sobbing, hysterically. Finally, she shook free of them and bolted into the woods, waving her arms and still screaming.

Bayardo shrugged sheepishly and nodded toward the door of one of the workers' shacks. "The cook is sick," he said. "She is concerned."

Sick? The cook was a German named Bern, and he had beaten me at chess only the night before. How sick could he be? "Oh, he is sick more or less," said Bayardo, trying to block my path to the door of the shack.

Did he need a doctor?

"No, I think that is not necessary."

Medicine?

"It is a thing we can ask in the morning, perhaps."

I could see Bern through the open door now. There was an oil lamp by the door—the maid had probably lighted it—and he was lying facedown, eyes open, hands like claws. Even on his best days, Bern wasn't what you would call handsome. Now he looked grotesque, and he didn't appear to be breathing.

"He doesn't look sick, Bayardo—he looks dead."

Averting his eyes, Bayardo said, "That is a possibility."

"Don't you think someone ought to check?"

He was suddenly embarrassed, and that's when I realized that neither Bayardo nor anyone else was going into that room at night, especially with the generator broken. I put the oil lamp on the little nightstand, grabbed Bern by the wrist, and flipped him over. He was still warm but there was no pulse, no respiration. Behind me, Bayardo, his head poked cautiously through the door, was saying, "These peasants, these stupid peasants, they are frightened of death—as if it might crawl up their arms and into their hearts. They will fix their own breakfast in the morning! And just what they deserve, refusing to touch a man on his deathbed."

That began a long night of searching the woods for the hysterical maid, of trying to calm her, of contacting the medical examiner by radio telephone, of waiting for the small plane to land in the pasture at daylight, of trying to force the by-then uncooperative Bern into the plane's lone passenger seat, of watching the plane bank away over the Pacific—a sight extraordinary for the open window Bern had required, and his frozen cavalier wave.

Later that day after the maid, Maria-Elaina, had been found and consoled that Bern had "left," she brought me a snack that Bern had apparently prepared for me before his sudden "departure." It was a delicious ceviche treat, *típico de* Costa Rica. I have named it "Dead Bern's Ceviche."

Enjoy! He would love that!—RWW

I was up at first light. A beautiful dawn. I sat on the fly bridge and watched the sun spreading over the eastern horizon, changing the earth. —*The Deep Six*, RWW (as Randy Striker)

Dead Bern's Ceviche

I met Bern in the jungle of Costa Rica. He gave me this great recipe shortly before he died. He was a really good chess player, too.—RWW

½ gallon of water

4 tablespoons salt

4 green bananas, peeled

2 pounds fish fillets, chunked

juice of 4 fresh lemons

cilantro to taste

2 medium onions, diced

2 green bell peppers, diced

Place a large pot filled with ½ gallon water over high heat. Add 4 tablespoons salt. (If the bananas are not cooked long enough and are still mushy like mashed potatoes, the salt helps them harden a little and maintain their form.) Bring to a boil and add green bananas. Boil green bananas for 10 minutes. Remove bananas from water and place in refrigerator to cool. When bananas are cool, cut them into quarters lengthwise and then crosswise into pie-shaped pieces about a centimeter thick.

Slice the fish into thin pieces about the size of a fish scale. Place fish in a large glass bowl. Add lemon juice and stir to mix, making sure juice completely covers fish. Cover bowl with cling wrap and refrigerate for 2 hours so that fish can cook in the lime juice.

Add bananas, cilantro, onions, bell peppers, and salt to taste. Toss to combine ingredients. Cover bowl and refrigerate for 2 to 3 hours more. Serve as a side dish or an appetizer served with tostados or saltine crackers. (Serve hot sauce and mayonnaise on the side, if you like.)

SERVES 4 TO 6.

Recipe courtesy of Randy Wayne White.

Carlene is the only woman to win the Fort Myers Beach Tarpon Hunter's Club Annual Open Division Tournament (twenty-four tarpon released). This was the only tarpon Carlene ever killed and, although she buried the fish in her yard under an almond tree and has a fiberglass mount of the fish above her fireplace, she wished she had released the silver king. Times were different in the 1970s and '80s. Most tarpon today are released to catch another day.

Sunset at Sanibel Island

CHAPTER 7

HERBS

I sat there reading in the soft light as a sulfur moth fluttered around, casting a pterodactyl shadow on ceiling and screen. Moonlight and the smell of night-blooming jasmine filtered in on dense air, as if fanned by the moth's wings. —*Shark River*, RWW

Cooking with Herbs

The recipes in this book calling for herbs or herb combinations vary from cook to cook, country to country, and island to island. The good cooks I know are all experimenters, both in selection and in quantities, and use recipes as suggestions rather than hard-and-fast rules. However, good cooks who wish to repeat good recipes know that a different herb combination will result in a different dish, even when all other ingredients are precisely the same. Be sure you keep a record in your memory or in a card file of just which (and how much) of each herb you used for those dishes that made such a splash on those special occasions.

Also remember that some herb combinations make especially happy marriages. Marjoram and summer savory, and thyme with parsley and marjoram (or both), happen to be very successful blends. There are many others that you can discover for yourself; for example, tarragon and cilantro for fish. I personally select from cilantro, thyme, bay, sage, oregano, marjoram, rosemary, tarragon, basil, savory, fennel, chervil, and cumin. Use fresh celery, parsley, shallots, scallions, onions, and garlic.

Incidentally, it is interesting to discover how the flavor of garlic changes according to the way it is cooked. Chopped and fried, it is very volatile, whereas whole cloves cooked gently for a long time become mild and buttery. —RWW

Herbed Carrots

Thyme is one of my favorite herbs to use when cooking fresh vegetables. But keep in mind—I don't like vegetables too much. —RWW

1 pound young carrots, washed and scrubbed

2 tablespoons butter, cut in small pieces

½ teaspoon thyme

½ teaspoon salt

Preheat grill. Cut carrots into ¼-inch-long angled slices. Place butter pieces evenly in the bottom of an aluminum-foil pouch or foil pan. Add carrots. Sprinkle carrots with thyme and salt. Fold pouch to seal tightly or cover foil pan tightly with aluminum foil. Place on grill for 20 to 30 minutes.

SERVES 4.

Recipe courtesy of Lynda Leonard-Boyce.

Red mangroves

The sun disrupted into molten gold upon Florida Bay, and the mangrove islands nearly looked frail but steadfast upon their small base . . . —*Everglades Assault,* RWW (as Randy Striker)

No human being should be allowed to die without watching sunrise at sea. —*The Deep Six*, RWW (as Randy Striker)

Tarpon Bay Marina docks

Herb-Grilled Grouper

Rosemary and basil make a wonderful combination when grilling fish. —RWW

vegetable cooking spray

1 pound grouper fillets

1 tablespoon olive oil

1 teaspoon chopped fresh rosemary

1½ tablespoons chopped fresh basil

2 tablespoons Key lime juice

salt and pepper

Preheat grill. Coat a large sheet of aluminum foil with vegetable cooking spray. Place fish fillets on foil and brush with olive oil. Sprinkle fillets with rosemary, basil, and Key lime juice. Season with salt and pepper to taste.

Seal foil envelope-style so that fillets are tightly enclosed. Place foil packet on grill. Cook 10 minutes or until fish flakes when tested with a fork.

Recipe courtesy of Carlene Fredericka Brennen.

SERVES 3.

Behind us, in our slow, expanding wake, the tiny clearing that was Dinkin's Bay Marina—wooden buildings, a few cars and docks, the Red Pelican Gift Shop, my house on pilings—was the only break in the great ring of mangroves. —*Everglades*, RWW

My Doc Ford's Fort Myers Rum Bar & Grille is located on historic Matanzas Pass, home of the Fort Myers Beach Shrimp Fleet.

CHAPTER 8

HOT SAUCES, SALSAS, AND CHUTNEYS

Dread of the abyss is communal among outdoor people. It is not the fear that unites us, but the potential that anything, absolutely anything, can happen. It creates a kind of congenial freemasonry—perhaps because feelings of dread, like nightmares, usually vanish when exposed to light. —*Twelve Mile Limit*, RWW

In Search of the Perfect Hot Sauce www.docford.com

Perfection is a goofball pursuit, one that's not only subjective but ultimately self-defeating: To find what you're looking for means the search has ended. Which is a shame, really, because roaming around looking for something is nearly always more fun than finding it. That's true of perfect waves and perfect countryside, and it's true—God help me—of perfect hot sauce.

And yet I may have fouled my own premise here, because I think I've found a hot sauce that's uncomfortably close to perfection. I discovered it at its place of origin, a large, open-air building of tin and wood near the suburb of Mamonel, southeast of Cartagena, Colombia, on the road to San Jacinto, where out-of-work cartel guerrillas have lately turned their skills to the profitable business of kidnapping travelers or popping drivers in the head for quick cash.

But that comes later in the story. First you need to understand a few things about my interest in pepper plants and my search for the perfect hot sauce. In 1987, on my way to Australia, I spent a little time in Fiji. One day around noon, I put on running shoes and went for a jog through the steamy streets of Suva, the capital city. Halfway through my run a tiny Indian man pulled his car off the road, hopped out, and called to me: "Sir, are you an American?" The insinuation was obvious: only an American would be foolish enough to run at noon. I nodded that I was an American, then listened dumbly as the man approached me and, without offering the slightest introduction or briefest preamble, said, "Oh, thank God I've met you. I've just been married, and an American will know. Please tell me, sir—what can a man do to cure premature satisfaction?"

This poor man was convinced that his discomfiture was a symptom of being oversexed and that he was oversexed because of a cultural dependence on spicy food. Hot peppers, he told me, were well-known aphrodisiacs. He'd been eating them in one form or another since infancy. "It was in my mother's milk, I tell you!"

His family grew its own peppers—a variety of *Capsicum annuum* peppers, similar to jalapeños, which he called by his own name—Bombay something-or-other—and he was addicted to the things. "I eat them all day, and it has warped my thinking," the man told me. "It is difficult to concentrate at my work. I can think of nothing but sex! I am like a machine!" He paused for a moment and made a small amendment: "A very, very fast machine. It is driving me mad. I love my wife very much, and we are both desperate. Isn't there some type of pill that you use in America?"

No, I said, but it seemed to me he was ignoring the obvious solution. "Why don't you stop eating all those hot peppers?" I asked.

It was at that instant, standing beneath a shade tree along the streets of Suva, that for the first time I received the peculiar dopester's stare of what in these faddish times is known as a chili-head. It was a frenzied look, as if I'd yanked a feeding heron up by the neck and held it eye to eye.

"Give up hot food?" he said. "For what—a woman?"

Yes, he may have been a very practical reason: I wanted some of those peppers. Yes, he may have been a crazed and offensive man, but I honored him—and for a very practical reason: I wanted some of those family peppers. I later persuaded him to give me a couple of them to take back to the States. After I got home I planted the seeds in the garden behind my house just to see if they would grow.

They did. They were pretty plants, too, producing a banana-shaped fruit that turned green, then yellow, then red. Looking at those plants made me think of running in Fiji and of the troubled man with his new wife, and it also caused me to project the long path those seeds had traveled: all the way from some little village near Bombay, probably across the Indian Ocean, past Australia to the South Pacific, and then around the rest of the world to my garden on the west coast of Florida.

That was the beginning of my search for the perfect hot sauce and the perfect pepper. It was not a difficult thing to collect seeds as I traveled to the far reaches of the world, and whenever I returned from a trip I would plant them.

A couple of summers ago, I walked a pepper fancier through my little garden. He was an Alcoa-lipped brand of chili-head, which is to say that the hotter the peppers, the better he pretended to like them. He came to the little red chili pequenos I'd pilfered from a bush in the Bahamas. "These are nice," he said. "I've always liked these. Crush them up, they're good in beer." He was tossing the things down like M&Ms.

Then we came to the two short rows that contain what I now know are *C. chinense* varieties. I keep them separate from the peppers I actually use because they don't have much taste and they're way too hot. Among them were several chunky black peppers from Southeast Asia that I myself had never had the courage to try.

"You won't believe the heat in these peppers!" said the farmer from Jalapa, Mexico, possible birthplace of the jalapeño. "A wild and ancient heat that touches the soul!" The chili-head nonchalantly picked one of the black peppers and popped it into his mouth, and then his face began to change. It is said that the human eye does not convey emotion. Whoever said that hasn't watched a man recklessly eat a variety of *C. chinense*. The ocular lens cannot wrinkle, but it can bulge as if registering some hellish internal pressure, and that's exactly what I saw in the eyes of this chili-head.

"Mother of God!" he whispered when he could finally form words. "Man . . . that's good!"

I've never participated in these silly machismo ceremonies, which require the hot-pepper eater to pretend he isn't in severe pain. Nor have I ever been interested in hot sauces that require users to dole out portions with an eyedropper. But collecting pepper seeds and bottles of hot sauce has become an obsessive hobby of mine. I've grown to like the way certain chilies taste and smell, and I'm deeply fascinated by their long and oddly convoluted history. I've come to greatly enjoy the slow glow that originates at the mouth and spreads north and south (which may be why some believe they're an aphrodisiac).

Now, whenever I'm cooking, or whenever I'm standing out in my garden, I can relive all kinds of trips: Cuba, Australia, Jamaica, Indonesia, Thailand, and lots of other places where people grow and use the little darlings, and that includes just about every region on earth.

A lesson in travel is what hot peppers are. Ask a schoolchild what Christopher Columbus discovered in 1492, and he or she will say the Americas. Ask a chili-head, and the response will be "capsicums."

Capsicum is a genus of waxy fruits—all containing the potent alkaloid capsaicin—that are indigenous to a large tropical swath of the New World ranging from Amazonia all the way to Mesoamerica. These plants were called *chil* by the Aztecs, and they have been on the move ever since. According to some archaeologists, the indigenous people of the New World have been cultivating and eating hot peppers for 6,500 years. When Columbus landed, capsicums were vital to the diet of many of the Native Americans he met. In a log from his second voyage, Columbus wrote of chilies that the "Caribs and Indians eat that fruit as we eat apples." In 1492, there were fewer than half a dozen species of capsicum being cultivated in the Americas. In subsequent years, European explorers collected two principal species of peppers—*C. annuum* and *C. chinense*—from what is now the West Indies and Central and South America, and steadily distributed them around the world.

What was once a spice has nowadays become a way of life. There are hundreds of hot-pepper societies around the world and hundreds of thousands of die-hard chili-heads who network on chili home pages on the World Wide Web. The present boom in the United States got started sometime back in the 1980s, and it's proven to be one of those exceedingly durable trends, like fly fishing and single-malt scotch, that won't let up. Not that I've paid much attention. My own interest in the subject continues to be random and solitary, though increasingly informed. Recently, for instance, I learned that my Indian friend in Fiji wasn't the first person to believe that hot peppers are aphrodisiacs. According to Jean Andrews's excellent book, *Peppers: The Domesticated Capsicums* (University of Texas Press), this myth got started sometime in the late 1500s when Father José de Acosta, a missionary, warned that their use "is prejudicial to the health of young folks, chiefly to the soul, for that it provokes to lust."

Chilies may be lust-provoking (we chili eaters certainly hope so), but the missionary was sadly mistaken in calling them "prejudicial to the health." We now know that one medium-size green chili pepper contains 130 percent of the recommended daily allowance of vitamin C—a higher concentration than that found in citrus fruit. It's also known that capsicums can help prevent dangerous blood clots. There's increasing evidence that hot peppers can reduce inflammatory responses, including those in burns, some nerve disorders, and arthritis.

Researchers at the National University of Singapore have even made claims that certain chilies can protect stomach cells against damage caused by alcohol, and that they may also prevent ulcers.

Not only that, but medical research has also confirmed something dedicated chili eaters have known all along: that we, in fact, enjoy an emotional "high." The burning sensation caused by peppers triggers the manufacture of endorphins, the body's own painkillers. The euphoria is similar to that enjoyed by long-distance runners and other endurance athletes who have yet to learn that they could feel just as good by curling up with a cold six-pack and a couple of habaneras.

There is no country on earth, I have discovered, that is too poor to cultivate chilies, and there is no citizenry so downtrodden that it will not cheerfully discuss and exaggerate the merits of its own local stock.

In the mountain city of Jalapa, Mexico—where it is widely believed that jalapeños originated—I obtained from a local man a small bag of what he said were seeds from the "original and authentic" jalapeño plant that only his family now possessed.

"My family has treasured and protected these pepper plants for at least two hundred years," he told me. "Maybe more. You will not believe the heat in these peppers. It is a wild and ancient heat that touches the soul!"

Chilies may indeed touch the soul, but they contribute little to the intellect, as I once discovered during a trip to Vietnam. In the Central Highlands, I hired a car and driver to take me from Pleyku to Saigon. The Vietnamese are a great people, but their driving skills were handed down by a consortium of drunken French colonialists and former MiG fighter pilots, the net result being that the country's mountain roads are death traps.

My own driver was typical—a speed demon blithely unimpressed by the prospect of road carnage. Then I noticed a tiny bag of purplish black chilies on the seat beside me. I suddenly imagined that I had a kinship with this lead-footed man: We shared the same obsession. If I could turn our journey into a collegial hunt for pepper seeds, I thought, perhaps my driver would back off the accelerator just a little.

I let him know what I wanted. His reaction was enthusiastic. Yes, he knew just where I could find some seeds from an incredibly hot black Vietnamese pepper— and then he mashed the gas pedal to the floor.

I knew of only a couple of useful phrases in Vietnamese (for instance, *Toi khong phai Uguoi nga*—"I am not a Russian"), but I knew enough about the country's drivers to ask a Vietnamese-American friend back in Hanoi what to say when I wanted to go slower.

Now I spoke the word: "*Nhanh . . . Nhanh!*"

My driver chuckled and we skidded through the next curve, going just as fast as we could go.

I tried again, yelling, "*NHANH! NHANH!*"

No response. We flew over hills and through villages, scattering curly-tailed dogs and cyclists and idiotic chickens.

Getting the man to slow down was hopeless, so I finally crawled over the seat and lay on the floor, resigned to the inevitable crash.

Yet we didn't crash. We found some pepper seeds, we made it to Saigon, and it wasn't until days later that I learned that my evil friend—thinking it was funny—had intentionally given me the wrong word for "slow."

"You dolt," my friend explained, "*nhanh* means 'faster.'"

"Great joke," I told him. "Hey, try one of those black peppers. They're mild as Nebraska squash."

I've planted and grown many chilies over the years, but in my travels I've taste-tested only several dozen of the hundreds of pepper sauces that are available around the world. Here are some hot sauces that are available around the world. Here are some hot sauces that I liked a lot, or at least that I found especially memorable: Red Extracto from Nicaragua; Majestica Hot Sauce from Singapore; Twin Elephants from Thailand; Tamarindo Pepper Sauce from Costa Rica; Congo Picante from Panama; Salsa Verde Picante from Cuba.

But recently, traveling through Colombia, I came across a local concoction that I believe was the best hot sauce I've ever tried. It was a pungent green, quite hot but not too hot. It had the fragrance of rich vinegar and crushed pepper blooms. It was simple. It was pure. Its name was Aji Amazona.

For me, successful travel requires serendipitous intersectings, and that's just what happened in Colombia. I was staying on the island of Manga, just off Cartagena, at a great little marina called Club Nautico. When I remarked upon the sauce, the marina's owner, an expatriate Aussie, replied, "Yeah—pretty good stuff, isn't it? I happen to know the guy who makes it."

Their little factory, Comexa, was a short taxi ride away from the marina, so I went to buy a case. I also met the proprietor, Jorge Araujo. "If you want to learn about peppers," Araujo told me, "I will show you."

Araujo took me out to the lush farming region where locals raised the chili peppers from which the hot sauce was made. As he drove, he remarked on the serious problems the area had been having with guerrilla kidnappers and bandits. Earlier that week, two German tourists had been robbed and murdered. I'd also heard that Colombian guerrillas were kidnapping as many as a thousand people a year, holding them for ransom.

Araujo said he knew nothing about this, though he did note that we weren't far from an area that "is not so safe." But all I saw were bright green fields and quiet villages and grinning children. Locals were selling buckets of wild honey,

I have found a hot sauce close to perfection!

mangoes, and boxes of tamarind pods. Farmers were loading peppers, which would be packed with vinegar in tight wooden kegs and left to age for a year before processing.

Araujo told me that he had been in the wholesale pepper business, supplying produce to larger companies, when a "miracle" happened: an accidental cross-pollination. "In the fields," he said, "our growers had cayenne peppers, but they also had a local variety called pipon, a big, red, stomachy variety that no manufacturer really wanted."

The pepper that resulted from this fortuitous cross-pollination was a rare specimen indeed. "It had a wonderful smell to it and a very bright color like no other I'd even seen," said Araujo. "We called it the Accidental Pepper. But what could we do with it? We decided to try and make our own sauces."

Eventually Jorge christened this accidental hybrid the "Amazona." Named for the region where all chilies probably originated, it now follows its pre-Columbian ancestors on newer trade routes.

"Have you tried it?" Jorge asked.

I'd sampled the sauce back in Cartagena, I said, but I hadn't yet taken a bite of the actual pepper. And truth be told, I wasn't sure I wanted to. For all I knew, it could be perfect.

—*Last Flight Out, "Dr. Pepper,"* RWW

Hot sauces from these peppers are available on my website, www.docford.com:

Doc Ford's Green Flash

Captiva Sunrise Mojo Rojo

Tomlinson's Colombian Gold

Tomlinson's No Mas! Habanero

Doc Ford's Salsa Chipotle

The Hot Sauce Team in Cartagena, including my lovely wife, Wendy

Pineapple Chutney

Most people associate pineapples with Hawaii, but they're also a traditional Florida crop. In the early 1900s, pineapples were grown commercially on Sanibel and nearby Pine Island. I still enjoy sprouting the tops I've cut from fresh pineapples, planting them, and watching them grow. —RWW

4 cups cored and chopped fresh pineapple (about 1½ fully ripened pineapples)

1 cup raisins

⅓ cup cider vinegar

⅓ cup chopped sweet onions, like Vidalia

¼ cup fresh lemon juice

2 tablespoons chopped crystallized ginger

2 teaspoons salt

½ teaspoon ground cloves

1 teaspoon ground allspice

½ teaspoon ground cinnamon

½ teaspoon ground ginger

1 (3-ounce) box Certo fruit pectin

½ teaspoon butter or margarine

4 cups sugar

Place pineapple in a 6- to 8-quart saucepan over high heat. Stir in raisins, vinegar, onions, lemon juice, crystallized ginger, salt, cloves, allspice, cinnamon, and ground ginger. Add Certo, stirring to mix well. Add butter and bring to a full rolling boil, stirring constantly. Quickly stir in sugar, return mixture to a full boil, and boil for 5 minutes, stirring constantly, so that mixture does not scorch. Remove saucepan from heat and skim off any foam with metal spoon.

Quickly ladle pineapple mixture into hot, sterilized 8-ounce jars, filling to within ⅛ inch of the top. Wipe jar rims and threads. Cover with the 2-piece lid, screwing bands tightly. Process in a boiling-water bath for 7 minutes to seal.

MAKES 3 PINTS.

Recipe courtesy of Lynda Leonard-Boyce.

Bonita Bill's Salsa

One of my favorite places to eat and drink is a bayside café that almost no one knows about, and where only locals go. It's in the old shrimp yards of Matanzas Pass, a funky, quirky outdoor restaurant and bar built beneath the sky bridge that joins Fort Myers Beach with tiny San Carlos Island. It's called Bonita Bill's and it may be the only restaurant in Florida with an unlisted number.—Everglades, RWW

2 ears fresh sweet corn with husks

7 medium tomatoes, seeded and diced

3 medium green bell peppers, cored, seeded, and diced

2 large red bell peppers, cored, seeded, and diced

2 onions, chopped

2 to 3 jalapeños, seeded and minced

1 whole bulb garlic, cloves peeled and minced

½ cup chopped fresh cilantro

juice of 1 lime

1 teaspoon salt

2 teaspoons cumin

Doc Ford's Green Flash Hot Sauce (available at www.docford.com)

Preheat grill. Wet cornhusks thoroughly. Place corn on grill and roast, turning occasionally, until cooked through. Remove corn from grill and allow it to cool. When corn is cool, cut kernels from cob.

Place corn, tomatoes, bell peppers, onions, jalapeños, garlic, and cilantro in a large glass bowl. Toss ingredients to mix. Add lime juice, salt, cumin, and hot sauce. Toss to mix well. Cover bowl with cling wrap and refrigerate for at least 2 hours to marry flavors. Serve with tortilla chips. (Roasting the bell peppers, onions, and garlic adds a different twist to this salsa.)

MAKES ABOUT 3 TO 4 CUPS.

Recipe courtesy of Bonita Bill's Waterfront Café on San Carlos Island and
K. S. Young and A. L. Rainey of *A Back Bay Look at Culinary Delights.*

Bonita Bill's is one of the greatest bars in Florida!—RWW

The most striking creatures—were the butterflies. They would come fluttering into the river gloom, catch a stray of light, and burst into bright flames of iridescent lavender or gold, then veer back into the shadows, the light still clinging to their wings. —*The Best of Outside*, RWW

Mango Chutney

If you think you don't like mangoes, it's because you've only tried the stringy, pine-tar-tasting varieties too often sold in supermarkets. They're terrible—but don't give up. Every August, Pine Island (right across the bay from Sanibel) hosts the International Mango Festival—dozens of varieties of mangoes are grown here. Some varieties are delicious; others superb; a few are ambrosia. I hold mango tastings on my porch. This chutney is a fave. —RWW

1 teaspoon cumin

5 jalapeños, seeded and minced

¼ clove garlic, minced

3 apricots, diced

2 teaspoons sugar

1 large mango, peeled, seeded, and diced

¼ teaspoon nutmeg

2 teaspoons lime juice

2 teaspoons cayenne pepper

1 teaspoon chopped fresh cilantro

Place all ingredients in a medium glass bowl. Toss to mix. Cover bowl with cling wrap and refrigerate for at least 1 hour or until ingredients are chilled. Serve over pork, use as a barbecue sauce for chicken, or serve over grilled fish.

MAKES ABOUT 1 CUP.

Recipe courtesy of K. S. Young and A. L. Rainey of *A Back Bay Look at Culinary Delights.*

. . . there was the smell of heat and vegetation like wood ash and warm lime peelings, an odor that was pure Florida. —*Sanibel Flats,* RWW

Red Pelican Gift Shop
at Tarpon Bay Marina

The first Sanibel Causeway,
now all but a memory

Carlene with two good-size spotted sea trout

Tropical Fruit Salsa

This dish is a wonderful complement to my fresh-caught snapper or grouper and has been featured on the menu of the charming Sunshine Seafood Café on Captiva Island. —RWW

1 medium red bell pepper, cored, seeded, and diced

2 medium green bell peppers, cored, seeded, and diced

1 medium red onion, chopped

2 large tomatoes, seeded and diced

1 bunch scallions, chopped

2 medium jalapeños, seeded and minced (optional)

1 medium papaya, peeled, seeded, and diced

1 medium mango, peeled, seeded, and diced

1 carambola (star fruit), diced

1 bunch fresh cilantro, finely chopped

1 cup olive oil

¼ cup red wine vinegar

1½ teaspoons salt

1 teaspoon pepper

1 teaspoon Tabasco sauce

2 teaspoons cumin

1½ tablespoons chili powder

Place all ingredients in a large glass bowl and toss to combine. Cover bowl with cling wrap and refrigerate at least 1 hour or until ingredients are chilled. Serve with grilled fish, chicken, or pork.

SERVES 8.

Recipe courtesy of Sunshine Seafood Café on Captiva Island.

Grilled Grouper Wrapped in Prosciutto on Bed of Salsa

This was a popular item on the menu at the Palm Ridge Café on Sanibel. A memory from the past. —RWW

6 tomatoes, blanched, peeled, cored, seeded, and finely chopped

1 clove garlic, minced

1 red bell pepper, cored, seeded, and finely chopped

1 green bell pepper, cored, seeded, and finely chopped

2 jalapeños, seeded and minced

2 tablespoons olive oil

½ bunch cilantro, finely chopped

½ teaspoon cumin

1 red onion, chopped

salt and pepper

4 (8-ounce) grouper fillets

12 ounces prosciutto, thinly sliced

Place tomatoes, garlic, bell peppers, jalapeños, olive oil, cilantro, cumin, and onion in a large glass bowl. Toss to mix ingredients. Season with salt and pepper to taste. Toss again. Cover bowl with cling wrap and refrigerate at least 1 hour to chill.

Preheat grill. Wrap each grouper fillet with 3 ounces prosciutto. Coat prosciutto with vegetable cooking spray. Grill over medium heat for 10 minutes per side.

Divide salsa among 4 dinner plates. Place 1 prosciutto-wrapped grilled grouper fillet atop each serving.

SERVES 4.

Brown pelican at Redfish Pass on Captiva

Canoeing at Tarpon Bay

CHAPTER 9

OYSTERS, CLAMS, AND MUSSELS

The oyster bars deflected water into abrupt tidal cauldrons that slurped and coiled with the speed of the tide. —*The Heat Islands*, RWW

Oysters—One of My Favorite Foods

People who are devoted to physical integrity and personal fitness may find the sedentary life aboard a train irksome—even I was beginning to feel a little stodgy. So when it was announced that we would have a two-hour layover in New Orleans, I put on shorts and running shoes and jogged out of Union Terminal, past the Superdome, toward the French Quarter. But running at midday in New Orleans is not easy. The air is as heavy as hot silk, and every block is spiced with the odor of a different restaurant, each a temptation. After about ten minutes of intensive exercise, I decided I had earned a light meal so, on St. Charles Street, I stepped into the Pearl Restaurant, a working-class bistro with linoleum floors, high ceiling fans, and a lunch counter.

Chuck was working behind the bar, and he recommended oysters. I had a dozen raw. Chuck observed that it was a shame I didn't have time to try the fried oysters, because they were very good, too. I did have time, so I had a dozen of those, plus a bottle of local beer, Dixie Amber Light. I sat there eating and talking

with Chuck (people at the Pearl were wonderfully chatty—uncommon in big-city restaurants), so I chose to prolong my stay by ordering a plate of red beans. Chuck served the beans smoking hot, with corn bread and a thick-cut sausage, and he placed another iced bottle of beer on the counter. After the beans, I was trying to choose between an order of seafood gumbo or Miss Leola's jambalaya when Chuck mentioned that they had just taken a bucket of Cajun boiled potatoes from the cooler, and would I like to try a couple on the house?

I was midway through my second potato, still conversing with Chuck, when I happened to notice that the clock on the wall didn't match the watch on my wrist. To my horror, I realized that the night before, I had mistakenly backed my watch two hours, not one, when adjusting for the time-zone change. Now, instead of having more than an hour to get back to the train, I had less than ten minutes. With the barest of explanations, I threw a wad of money on the counter and bolted into the heat. To make the train, I would have to sprint the whole way, but I couldn't sprint for long, not after the lunch I had just eaten. Indeed, just breathing was uncomfortable. Even so, I struggled along, probably looking like some godforsaken refugee with my distended belly and Quasimodo gait. At the Superdome, I steeled myself and ran the rest of the way to Union Terminal and arrived just in time to hear, "Last call for the Sunset Limited!"

There were two long lines of people, tickets in hand, waiting to be checked into the boarding area, but I ran seemingly unnoticed right past them and the ticket punchers, proving perhaps that joggers have finally joined the ranks of winos and stray dogs as invisible creatures of the street.

As I closed my cabin door, the train began to jolt, then gather speed, and moments later, Mr. Graham knocked, then asked, "You want me to bring lunch to your cabin?"

I said, "Dear God, no." Even the slightest movement on my part, I feared, would introduce Mr. Graham to the lunch I had just eaten. [Although Chuck's marvelous oysters were my undoing at the beginning of the extraordinary meal, oysters still remain one of my favorite foods.]

—*The Sharks of Lake Nicaragua,* "A Train, America and a Frog," RWW

Scalloped Oysters

Oysters are a wonderful food no matter how you prepare them. I like to wade oyster bars, on winter low tides, with a lime in hand. Shuck one, then put a few in the bucket. —RWW

1 pint shucked oysters

2 cups medium-coarse cracker crumbs

½ cup butter or margarine, melted

pepper

¾ cup light cream

¼ cup oyster liquor

¼ teaspoon Worcestershire sauce

½ teaspoon salt

Preheat oven to 350°F. Drain oysters, reserving liquor. Place cracker crumbs and butter in a medium bowl and stir to combine. Spread one-third of the crumbs in a greased 8 x 1¼-inch round baking pan. Place half the oysters atop the crumbs. Sprinkle with pepper. Spread another one-third of crumbs over oysters. Place remaining oysters atop crumbs. Sprinkle with pepper.

Place cream, oyster liquor, Worcestershire sauce, and salt in a small bowl. Whisk to combine. Pour mixture over the oysters. Top with remaining cracker crumbs. Bake for 40 minutes.

SERVES 4.

Recipe courtesy of Randy Wayne White.

Oyster Cocktails

A favorite food at marina parties accompanied by a pitcher of my favorite margaritas. —RWW

Cocktail Sauce:

¾ cup chili sauce

2 to 4 tablespoons fresh lemon juice

2 to 3 tablespoons prepared horseradish

2 teaspoons Worcestershire sauce

1 teaspoon grated onion

3 drops Doc Ford's Chipotle Hot Sauce (available at: www.docford.com)

1 pint shucked oysters, or 36 oysters on the half shell (have seafood market open shells)

6 iceberg lettuce leaves

crushed ice

Place chili sauce, lemon juice, horseradish, Worcestershire sauce, onion, and hot sauce in a small bowl. Stir to combine. Refrigerate for at least 1 hour to chill.

For shucked oysters:

Place a lettuce leaf in each of 6 martini glasses. Drain oysters. Divide oysters evenly between 6 glasses, placing oysters atop lettuce leaves. Top each with a generous dollop of cocktail sauce.

SERVES 6.

For oysters on the half shell:

Remove and toss away upper flat shells of oysters. Loosen oysters from deep half shells with an oyster knife and remove shell bits. Replace oysters into the deep half shell. Refrigerate oysters until ready to serve. To serve, place a bed of crushed ice in each of 6 shallow, rimmed dishes. Place 6 oysters (on the half shell) atop each bed of ice. Place a dollop of cocktail sauce atop each oyster.

SERVES 6.

Recipe courtesy of Randy Wayne White.

Oysters Creole

Enjoy a chilled bottle of your favorite Chablis while adding some to the recipe when you prepare this tasty appetizer. —RWW

1 medium tomato, cored and diced

1 red bell pepper, cored, seeded, and diced

1 green bell pepper, cored, seeded, and diced

½ pound bacon, blanched in boiling water for 3 minutes, drained, and diced

½ cup diced onions

1 teaspoon fresh thyme

½ teaspoon cayenne pepper

½ teaspoon chili powder

½ teaspoon pepper

½ teaspoon salt

½ teaspoon garlic powder

⅓ cup Chablis wine

16 Blue Point coldwater oysters, shucked, 16 deep shells reserved

Preheat oven to 375°F. Place all ingredients except oysters in a large skillet over medium heat. Sauté, stirring frequently, for 2 to 3 minutes. Place an oyster in each of the 16 shells and top with tomato-pepper mixture. Place oyster shells on a baking sheet and bake for 6 to 8 minutes or until heated through.

SERVES 4.

Recipe courtesy of The Jacaranda on Sanibel Island.

The sea was a deafening darkness. In the far distance, the lighthouse was awash in monstrous clouds, each frail starburst reflected skyward, then absorbed as if ingested. —*Dark Light,* RWW

(Clockwise from top left) An osprey prepares to land in its nest. No island is complete without the presence of the raccoon. Sanibel had one resident crocodile in the J. N. "Ding" Darling National Wildlife Refuge for many years, but she has passed away. She is truly missed.

Clams Marinara

Clams never tasted better than with this combination of ingredients but it is the dry vermouth that gives this dish its signature taste. —RWW

    ¼ cup olive oil

    1 teaspoon minced garlic

    12 clams in the shell, scrubbed

    ¼ cup dry vermouth

    ½ cup marinara sauce

    grated Parmesan cheese

Place olive oil in an 8-inch, skillet over medium-high heat. When oil is hot, add garlic and sauté, about 1 minute, until aromatic.

Discard any clams with open shells. Add clams and vermouth to skillet. Cover and simmer 2 to 3 minutes or until clams open. Add marinara sauce and continue to simmer for 2 more minutes or until sauce is heated through. Transfer to a rimmed dish and sprinkle with Parmesan cheese to taste. Serve with toasted garlic bread.

SERVES 1.

Recipe courtesy of The Lazy Flamingo (two locations) on Sanibel Island.

The half moon was waxing, but the jungle seemed to lure then absorb all light, so that the frail moon above only emphasized the darkness. —*Sanibel Flats*, RWW

Seafood Linguine with Marinara Sauce

This is a signature dish at The Jacaranda on Sanibel. What a marvelous way to prepare seafood.
—RWW

1 (28-ounce) can plum tomatoes with juice

4 tablespoons olive oil

4 tablespoons minced garlic

¼ cup plus 1 teaspoon snipped fresh basil

1 medium onion chopped

salt and pepper

1 pound Dungeness or snow crab clusters

6 littleneck clams in shell

6 New Zealand mussels in shell

6 jumbo shrimp, peeled and deveined

1 pound linguine, cooked al dente per package instructions

2 tablespoons grated Parmesan cheese

Place tomatoes in a 2-quart saucepan and crush with the back of a wooden spoon. Add olive oil, garlic, ¼ cup snipped basil, onion, and salt and pepper to taste. Place saucepan over medium heat and bring mixture to a simmer, stirring occasionally.

Reduce heat to low, cover, and simmer for 2 hours, stirring occasionally.

Transfer marinara sauce to a 4-quart saucepan and place it over medium-low heat. When sauce is bubbly, add shellfish and steam until clam and mussel shells open, shrimp are pink, and crab is heated through. Add linguine and cook for 1½ minutes or until pasta is hot. Serve in large pasta bowls. Garnish with Parmesan cheese and the remaining 1 teaspoon fresh basil.

SERVES 4.

Recipe courtesy of The Jacaranda on Sanibel Island.

Scallops Provençal

Luckily I live in a state where you can get fresh scallops every day. This recipe is easy to prepare, and it will impress your guests. —RWW

¼ cup flour

1 pound Florida bay scallops, rinsed and patted dry

3 tablespoons olive oil

3 cloves garlic, minced

2 cups snow peas (about ½ pound)

2 cups sliced red bell peppers

1 cup sliced mushrooms

Place flour on a large plate. Roll scallops in flour.

Place oil in a large wok or skillet over medium-high heat. Add scallops and garlic and sauté until scallops are cooked through, about 5 to 10 minutes. Add snow peas, bell peppers, and mushrooms and stir-fry until vegetables are heated through but still crisp. Serve over wild or flavored rice.

SERVES 4.

Recipe courtesy of Lynda Leonard-Boyce.

Marinated Mussel Mini-Brochettes or Salad

Chef Brian Kershen, who lives on Useppa Island, is the creator of this wonderful dish. I love this meal with a glass of chilled white Australian wine, while sitting on my deck watching the sunset over Cayo Costa. —RWW

Marinade:

¼ cup white wine vinegar

¼ cup cider vinegar

¼ cup canola oil

¼ cup olive oil

1 tablespoon minced shallots

1½ tablespoons minced garlic

1 tablespoon chopped fresh parsley

1 teaspoon dried thyme

½ teaspoon dried oregano

½ teaspoon pepper

2 teaspoons sugar

½ teaspoon salt

1 tablespoon Dijon mustard

juice of 1 lemon

Salad:

3 tablespoons butter or margarine

1 pound button mushrooms, cleaned and stems trimmed

1 cup white wine

1 cup chicken broth

3 pounds mussels, cleaned and debearded

2 cucumbers

2 orange bell peppers, cored, seeded, and cut into ¾-inch cubes

chopped lettuce

Yellow-crowned night heron at Indigo Trail, J. N. "Ding" Darling National Wildlife Refuge

Place all marinade ingredients in a medium glass bowl and whisk to mix well. Set aside.

Place butter in a large, heavy pot over medium heat. When butter has melted, add button mushrooms and increase heat to high. Sauté mushrooms, stirring frequently, for 2 to 3 minutes or until mushrooms have partially browned. Add white wine and chicken broth. Bring liquid to a simmer, then reduce heat to low and simmer for 10 minutes.

Meanwhile, discard any dead mussels. Remove mushrooms from broth with a slotted spoon and set aside. Increase heat to medium-high and bring broth to a full boil. Add mussels. Cover pot with lid and cook mussels for 2 minutes or until all the mussels have opened. Drain mussels in a colander and set aside to cool.

While mussels are cooling, peel cucumbers, then cut them in half lengthwise. Remove seeds and cut cucumbers into ¾-inch chunks.

Remove cooled mussels from their shells. Place mussels, mushrooms, and bell peppers in a large bowl and toss them with all but ⅓ cup of the marinade. Cover bowl with cling wrap and refrigerate for at least 1 hour. Add cucumbers and toss them with mussel mixture. Cover and refrigerate for an additional 15 minutes.

Drain mussel mixture in a colander. Arrange lettuce on a serving platter. Place remaining marinade in a small bowl and place in the center of the greens. Thread 1 mussel, 1 bell pepper cube, 1 cucumber chunk, and 1 mushroom on a toothpick. Repeat with remaining ingredients and place mini-brochettes atop greens. Serve mini-brochettes with marinade dipping sauce. (Alternately, mussel mixture can be tossed with lettuce and reserved marinade to create a seafood salad.)

SERVES A CROWD.

Recipe courtesy of Chef Brian Kershen.

Marina guide Captain Neville Robeson, fishing with his charter on Tarpon Bay

Night sailing: running with the speed of the nocturnal clouds. A windblown night, with bioluminescence feathering the breaking waves and throwing a wake of green fire behind the boat. All is darkness but for the reluctant stars and a few dim lights on the horizon. I am forever curious about such lights—the lights that mark the nocturnal strongholds of human existence in all desolate or rural places—and I pass the night away in speculation, admiring them all, wishing them luck, one by one. —*Batfishing in the Rainforest*, RWW

Great blue egret at Jensen's Twin Palm
Resort & Marina on Captiva

CHAPTER 10

SHRIMP, CRAB, AND LOBSTER

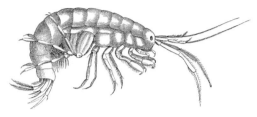

Anyone who says the underwater world is silent has never been underwater. As many times as I've hauled in trawl nets, I've yet to lose that feeling of anticipation and expectation before dumping that first strike from new bottom. You never know what might be inside . . . There were hundreds of fish, dozens of species: grunts, pinfish, flukes, cowfish, file fish, immature sea trout, croakers, gray snapper, lane snapper, thread herrings, immature female groupers, skipjacks, box fish, and southern puffers, the last two making rapid-fire inhalations as they inflated their bodies like miniature footballs. There were blue crabs and calico crabs, arrow crabs and hermit crabs. There were shrimp and sea horses, sea urchins, hydroids, and stingrays all buried among the grass and gumbo that smelled of iodine and fresh sea bottom, which is one of the most delicate and compelling odors I know. —*Shark River*, RWW

A Very Simple Shrimp Recipe

Joyce, who cooks in the seafood market (at Tarpon Bay Marina), uses a very simple recipe I brought back from Panama, compliments of some of my Zonie friends. Fill an empty wine bottle with virgin olive oil and a dozen or more chili peppers. Cork and allow it to age for at least a few weeks.

In a large bowl, pour the chili oil over fresh shrimp, squeeze in the juice of two fresh limes. Not lemons, limes. Salt heavily. Add garlic, black pepper, and, if you can find it, some Everglades Seasoning from Labelle for a nice Cuban touch. Allow the shrimp to marinate for a day. Cook them on a very hot grill. The oil creates a lot of flame and sears them nicely black. It only takes a minute or two on each side. Overcook the shrimp and they're ruined—dry and tough to peel. Get them off just as they turn pink and you've got one of the world's great culinary experiences. (Serve with fresh lime wedges, and mojitos.)

Which is why I'd heaped my plate high with shrimp. I sat there eating the shrimp, washing them down with iced beer, talking to the guides. Talking with the guides is a favorite pastime because they spend so much time on the water that any anomaly, any unusual experience, is immediately noted. Most light-tackle guides are keen observers and have an even keener sense of humor—a necessity in their very rough business. —RWW

Fresh-Cooked Shrimp

Washing down fresh boiled Florida shrimp with bottles of cold beer can make a good day better. —RWW

6 cups water

2 tablespoons salt

2 tablespoons vinegar

2 bay leaves

1 teaspoon mixed pickling spices

2 stalks celery, cut into 2-inch pieces

2 pounds fresh or frozen Florida pink shrimp, in the shell or peeled and deveined

Combine water, salt, vinegar, bay leaves, pickling spices, and celery; bring to boiling. Add shrimp, in shells or peeled and cleaned. Cover, heat to boiling, then lower the heat and simmer gently until shrimp turn pink, about 5 minutes. Drain. If cooked in shell, peel shrimp; remove vein that runs down back. For appetizer, chill; pass the cocktail sauce (see recipe, page 104).

MAKES 4 OR 5 SERVINGS.

Recipe courtesy of Randy Wayne White.

Joyce's Marina Grilled Shrimp

Most people overcook shrimp. The trick is to remove the shrimp from the grill as soon as they turn pink. —RWW

1½ pounds fresh Florida pink
    shrimp, in the shell

chili oil

juice from 2 limes

kosher or sea salt

garlic to taste

pepper

Everglades Seasoning

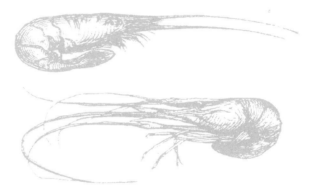

Place shrimp in a large glass or plastic container. Pour chili oil over shrimp so that oil just covers shrimp. Add lime juice. Add salt and garlic to taste. Season liberally with pepper and Everglades Seasoning. Toss to mix well. Cover, refrigerate, and marinate for 24 hours.

Preheat grill. Place shrimp on hot grill for 1 to 2 minutes. Turn shrimp and grill for 1 to 2 minutes more. Do not overcook.

SERVES 4.

Recipe courtesy of Randy Wayne White.

Shrimp fleet, San Carlos Island. Home of the Florida "Wild Pink Shrimp."

Joyce's French-Fried Shrimp

No matter how much I used live shrimp as bait for my charters, I never got tired of piling my plate full of Joyce's delicious fried shrimp. —RWW

1 cup sifted all-purpose flour

½ teaspoon sugar

½ teaspoon salt

1 egg, lightly beaten

1 cup ice water

2 tablespoons canola oil, plus more for deep-fat fryer

2 pounds fresh or frozen Florida pink shrimp, peeled with tail intact

2 lemons, cut into wedges

Place flour, sugar, salt, egg, water, and canola oil in a medium bowl. Beat with a wire whisk until smooth. Set aside.

Using a sharp knife, butterfly shrimp by cutting almost through the center back, without severing ends. Remove black vein. Rinse shrimp, then dry thoroughly with paper toweling.

Place manufacturer's recommended amount of canola oil in a deep-fat fryer and bring it to 375°F. Dip shrimp in batter and place in hot oil, frying until shrimp are golden brown. Drain shrimp on paper toweling. Serve immediately with lemon wedges and cocktail sauce (see recipe, page 104).

SERVES 4 TO 6.

Recipe courtesy of Randy Wayne White.

Tarpon Bay Shrimp

Tarpon Bay is full of the sweetest shrimp on the planet, so this recipe is rightly named. —RWW

2 teaspoons butter

12 jumbo Florida pink shrimp, peeled and deveined

garlic to taste

2 tablespoons chopped fresh basil

½ cup white wine

2 teaspoons beef broth or demi-glace

Place butter in a large skillet over medium heat. When butter has melted, add shrimp and sauté until shrimp are lightly browned on both sides, stirring frequently. Add garlic and basil and sauté 1 more minute. Add wine and beef broth and cook for 2 more minutes. Serve over rice.

SERVES 2.

Recipe courtesy of The Jacaranda on Sanibel Island.

It's not true about it being always darkest before the dawn. Not on the open ocean, anyway. There was no sun, but the sea took on a pearly luminance. The water changed from black to turquoise—a turquoise of such intensity that it seemed as if it would discolor the black hull of my cruiser. The wind freshened, blowing waves across the bow. And the rolling expanse of sea wind and waves seemed energized by an incandescence of its own, as if the radiance had been accumulated over a million days beneath the Gulf Stream sun. —*Cuban Death-Lift,* RWW (as Randy Striker)

About Doc Ford's Rum Bar & Grille

Welcome to my restaurant, Doc Ford's Sanibel Rum Bar & Grille (www
.docfordssanibel.com), located on beautiful Sanibel Island, Florida, at 975 Rabbit
Road. Before I started writing novels, I used to sell fish right at the site to a chef in
the building where my restaurant is now located.

For more than twelve years, I was a light-tackle fishing guide just down the
road at Tarpon Bay Marina. I did more than 3,000 charters; I spent 300 days a year
boating these waters. When my clients chose not to keep what they'd caught, I'd
load the fish in my pickup, tap on the back door of this place, and ask the chef if he
was in a buying mood.

I love the symmetry of that; I helped provide seafood here way back in the
1970s, and now, because I've joined this excellent team of restaurateurs and staff at
Doc Ford's, I have the opportunity to play a small role in providing fresh fish here
once again.

When you are in the neighborhood, stop by and say hello. Call ahead at (239) 472-8311 or e-mail us via the website at www.docfordsanibel.com. Just as my novels are inspired by these islands, my days on the water, and the people I came to know, the spirit of this fine sports bar was inspired by the marine biologist who is the main character of those novels.

Doc Ford is the baseball-loving, tropical adventurer who—not so surprisingly—has spent a lot of time in the same far-flung places that I wrote about when I was a monthly columnist for *Outside* magazine: places such as Cuba, Cambodia, South Africa, Australia, Vietnam, Borneo, and all over South and Central America. It was while traveling for *Outside* that I came to know and love the superb cuisine of the rural tropics.

I loved the sauces, the spices, and the passion that went into the food preparation. Many of these recipes I've shared with you in my cookbook. We hope that spirit is part of Doc Ford's Sanibel Rum Bar & Grille, too.

But the real hearts, heads, and souls behind my restaurant though, aren't fictional. They are real people; people savvy enough to envision a whole new concept in bars. A rum bar with gourmet finger foods. "Sports bars don't serve great food," we were told.

Well, this one does.

So credit Marty and Brenda Harrity, Mark and Heidi Marinello, and Jean Baer, along with Chef Greg Nelson for having the vision, and then finding the energy, taste, and chutzpah to make that vision reality. Being with them reminds me of my old marina family, back when I was a fishing guide at Tarpon Bay. They're quirky and fun and gifted. They've made it work, and I'm proud to have played a small part.

I wrote this text in 2006. Since then a lot has happened in my life, including my marriage to a beautiful singer/songwriter, Wendy Webb. I've written more Doc Ford novels, started another series about fishing guide Hannah Smith, and opened two more restaurants, Doc Ford's Fort Myers Beach Rum Bar & Grille on San Carlos Island, with marvelous waterfront views, and my latest establishment, Doc Ford's Captiva Rum Bar & Grille, nestled in a tropical garden atmosphere on beautiful Captiva Island, just a short drive from Sanibel. Life is good.—RWW

Green Curry Shrimp

This fantastic recipe came from my friend, Chef Brian Kershen, who lives close to my Pine Island home. The following is what he was kind enough to send to me. I have enjoyed his curried shrimp many times but never knew the exact recipe until now. Brian writes: "Quite often, when I am preparing food here on Useppa Island, my mind invariably wanders halfway around the globe to the cuisines of the Pacific Rim. I am a huge fan of Thai food, and this is my Americanized version of the popular Thai dish, Green Curry Shrimp. Some of the ingredients may seem exotic, but they are readily available at most large grocery stores in the Asian foods section." —RWW

3 tablespoons canola oil

1½ pounds fresh Florida pink shrimp, peeled and deveined

½ onion, cut into ½-inch cubes

1 green bell pepper, cored, seeded, and cut into thick strips

2 cups coarsely chopped cabbage

1 zucchini, cut in half and sliced into ½-inch chunks

1 tablespoon chopped garlic

1 cup chicken stock

1 (13½-ounce) can coconut milk

1 (8-ounce) can sliced bamboo shoots, drained

1 tablespoon Thai green curry paste

3 tablespoons Thai fish sauce

1 tablespoon sugar

1 teaspoon salt

juice of 1 lime

½ cup chopped fresh basil

Heat up a large pot over medium-high heat. Add oil. Toss shrimp into the oil and quickly stir-fry until just barely cooked. Remove shrimp with a slotted spoon. Add onion, green pepper, and cabbage to the pot and stir-fry for about 3 minutes. Add zucchini and garlic and sauté for 1 minute more. Add chicken stock, coconut milk, bamboo shoots, green curry paste, fish sauce, sugar, and salt, and cook on a low simmer for about 5 minutes. Add shrimp and cook for 1 minute more. Right before serving, squeeze in the juice of 1 lime. Ladle into bowls, top with fresh basil, and serve. (Note: Always serve with white rice, preferably jasmine rice, which has a nice aromatic quality to it.) This dish also works just as well as a chicken dish; just substitute 1 pound sliced chicken breast for the shrimp.

SERVES 4 TO 6.

Recipe courtesy of Chef Brian Kershen.

Shrimp Cocktail with Tequila Sauce

Tequila, no matter what brand, goes well with shrimp, whether in a sauce or in a cocktail accompanying the meal. —RWW

1 cup ketchup

1 cup chili sauce

⅓ cup prepared horseradish

2 tablespoons plus 2 teaspoons Worcestershire sauce

2 tablespoons lemon juice

2 teaspoons Doc Ford's Tomlinson's No Mas! Hot Sauce (available at: www.docford.com)

⅓ cup tequila

salt and pepper

4 pounds fresh Florida pink shrimp, deveined and in the shell

Place ketchup, chili sauce, horseradish, Worcestershire sauce, lemon juice, hot sauce, and tequila in a medium bowl. Whisk to combine. Season with salt and pepper to taste. Chill tequila sauce in refrigerator for at least 1 hour.

Place 4 cups water in a large saucepan over medium-high heat. When water has come to a boil, add shrimp. Cook for 2 to 3 minutes or until shrimp are just pink and still firm to the touch. Drain shrimp, place in a medium-size bowl, and refrigerate until chilled. Serve as peel-your-own with tequila sauce.

SERVES 2.

Recipe courtesy of Randy Wayne White.

Sunrise over Sanibel Fishing Pier

Coconut Shrimp

Carlene's daughter Shamie said this is one of the best coconut shrimp dishes she has ever tasted.
—RWW

1½ cups flour, divided

1¼ cups club soda

1 teaspoon baking powder

1 teaspoon baking soda

salt

2 pounds Florida pink shrimp, peeled and deveined

2 cups shredded unsweetened coconut

1 quart canola oil

Brown pelicans at Sanibel Marina

Place 1 cup of the flour, club soda, baking powder, baking soda, and a pinch of salt in a medium bowl. Whisk ingredients until batter is smooth. Dust shrimp with ½ cup of flour. Dip each shrimp into the batter, then place it on a baking sheet to drain for 5 minutes. Place coconut on a dinner plate. Roll battered shrimp in coconut.

Place canola oil in a deep-fat fryer. Heat oil to 325°F. Place shrimp in oil and fry until shrimp float in the oil and are golden brown. Remove shrimp and drain on paper toweling.

SERVES 2 TO 4.

Recipe courtesy of Gramma Dot's Seaside Saloon at Sanibel Marina on Sanibel Island.

Shrimp Perlo

A favorite of fishing crews and all who try it, this recipe has been passed down through generations of shrimpers to Captain Henry Gore of Fort Myers Beach. Henry is married to Carlene's niece Tracy, and, according to Carlene, is a marvelous cook. His shrimp dishes at family get-togethers are legendary, and you always know the shrimp is fresh. —RWW

- 1 (1-pound) package yellow rice mix
- 1 pound bacon, cut into small pieces
- 2 medium onions, finely chopped
- 1 pound Florida pink "wild" shrimp, peeled and deveined
- 4 (14½-ounce) cans stewed tomatoes

Cook rice in a large saucepan following package instructions. Meanwhile, place bacon in a large skillet over medium heat. Cook, stirring frequently, until bacon is partially cooked. Add onions and continue cooking, stirring frequently, until bacon is crispy and onions are translucent. Remove bacon and onions with a slotted spoon and drain on paper toweling.

Add bacon, onions, shrimp, and stewed tomatoes with juices to cooked rice. Stir to combine ingredients. Simmer over low heat for 20 minutes, or until shrimp have cooked through and sauce is hot.

SERVES 4.

Recipe courtesy of Captain Henry Gore.

Captain Henry Gore's Shrimp boat, *Doctor Tom*

Crab Cointreau

The blue crabs caught in Tarpon Bay produced some of the best crabmeat I ever tasted. —RWW

1 cup flaked, cooked (or canned) crabmeat, rinsed and drained

1 (10½-ounce) can of cream of mushroom soup

¼ cup heavy cream

2 tablespoons Cointreau

¼ cup seasoned bread crumbs

Preheat broiler. Place crabmeat, soup, cream, and Cointreau in a medium saucepan over low heat, stirring occasionally, until heated through. Divide crab mixture among individual ramekins. Top each portion with 1 tablespoon seasoned bread crumbs. Place under broiler until lightly browned.

SERVES 4.

Recipe courtesy of Lynda Leonard-Boyce.

Life among the offshore reef

All-Crab Crab Cakes

The fresh blue-crab meat with this marvelous remoulade sauce makes this recipe a real winner. —RWW

Remoulade Sauce:

½ cup mayonnaise

1 bunch fresh chives, chopped

juice of 1 lemon

2 tablespoons chopped capers

2 tablespoons chopped sweet gherkin pickles

1 hard-boiled egg, chopped

2 to 4 drops Tomlinson's Colombian Gold Hot Sauce (available at: www.docford.com)

Crab Cakes:

1 pound fresh jumbo lump blue-crab meat

1 tablespoon Dijon mustard

1 egg white

¾ teaspoon Old Bay Seasoning

salt and pepper

½ cup flour, seasoned to taste

2 tablespoons olive oil

For the remoulade sauce: Place mayonnaise, chives, lemon juice, capers, pickles, chopped egg, and hot sauce in a small bowl. Stir until ingredients are well mixed. Cover bowl with cling wrap and refrigerate until needed.

For the crab cakes: Pick through the crabmeat and remove any shell pieces. Place crabmeat, mustard, egg white, and Old Bay Seasoning in a medium bowl. Stir to combine ingredients. Season with salt and pepper to taste.

Form crabmeat mixture into four 1-inch-thick cakes. Place seasoned flour on a dinner plate. Dredge crab cakes in flour. Place olive oil in a large nonstick skillet over medium-high heat. When oil is hot, add crab cakes and sauté until golden brown, turning once. Serve with remoulade sauce.

SERVES 4.

Recipe courtesy of Captain Matt Mitchell of St. James City, Florida.

Crab Puffs

This recipe comes from friend Victor Mayeron, owner of The Mucky Duck on Captiva Island. A great restaurateur and raconteur. —RWW

1 teaspoon butter

¼ cup finely chopped onion

¼ cup finely chopped green bell pepper

¼ cup finely chopped celery

¼ cup cream sherry

1 pound crab claw meat, picked over

½ cup plain dried bread crumbs, divided

1 large egg, lightly beaten

⅛ teaspoon dry mustard

⅛ teaspoon cayenne pepper

⅛ teaspoon Old Bay Seasoning

⅓ cup mayonnaise

canola oil for deep-frying

Place butter in a large skillet over medium heat. When butter has melted, add onion, bell pepper, and celery and sauté, stirring frequently, until vegetables are just crisp. Add sherry and cook 2 more minutes. Remove skillet from burner and allow mixture to cool.

Place crab claw meat, ¼ cup bread crumbs, egg, mustard, cayenne pepper, Old Bay Seasoning, and mayonnaise in a large bowl. Stir to combine ingredients. Add onion mixture and stir to blend thoroughly.

Roll mixture into balls the size of golf balls. (If mixture is too sticky, add more crabmeat; if too dry, add a bit of mayonnaise.) Place remaining ¼ cup bread crumbs on a small plate. Roll crabmeat balls in crumbs to coat.

Place canola oil in deep-fat fryer per manufacturer's instructions. Heat to 375°F. Drop the crabmeat balls into the oil and fry for 3 to 5 minutes or until puffs are golden. Serve puffs with cocktail sauce or Dijon Mustard Sauce (see recipe, page 146).

SERVES 4.

Recipe courtesy of The Mucky Duck on Captiva Island.

I am not a baseball fan, but I'm a fan of baseball.
I have never followed teams or box scores, but I
love to play the game. —RWW

Florida Lobster

Diving for lobster in the Keys is a real kick. The only thing better is broiling your catch. —RWW

2 (1-pound) lobsters (select active, live lobsters if available)

8 tablespoons butter, melted

1 teaspoon seasoning salt

Broiled

Place lobster on its back. Pierce the spinal cord between the body and tail shells with a sharp knife. With knife, split lobster in half lengthwise. Discard craw or crop near head. Remove black vein that runs down to the tail. (Don't remove the green fat or red coral.) Flatten lobsters open on a broiler pan. Brush meat with melted butter. Season each lobster with ½ teaspoon seasoning salt.

Preheat broiler. Place lobsters under broiler. Broil for 12 to 15 minutes or until meat is no longer translucent when tested with a knife. Serve with melted butter.

Boiled:

Plunge headfirst into boiling, salted water to cover. Bring back to boiling; reduce heat, and simmer for 20 minutes. Remove at once. With sharp knife, cut in half lengthwise. Discard craw or crop near head, and remove black vein that runs to tip of tail. Crack claws.

Serve lobster as main course—hot with butter, or split and chilled with mayonnaise. Or remove meat for hot creamed dishes, casseroles, chilled salads, or appetizers.

Recipe courtesy of Randy Wayne White.

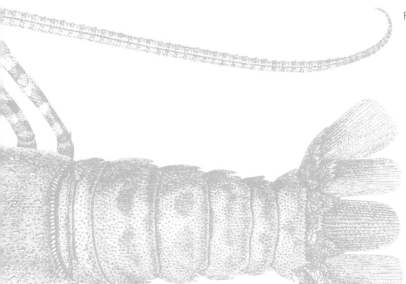

Center, with my shark charter at Tarpon Bay Marina. It's surprising how much these dead-fish-on-hook shots now trouble me—even though it was for the table, or taxidermy. —RWW

CHAPTER 11

SHARK AND OTHER FISH FROM THE GULF

[T]he moon disappeared behind the clouds, and I was speeding through mangrove shadow, hearing wind and water in the caverns of my ears. The bioluminescent wake I created was an expanding silver-green crescent. The sensory combination was that of riding a comet across a liquid universe. Off to my right, I saw a mobile galaxy of green streaks: a school of fish. I watched the school explode in a firestream of color; then explode again. —*Everglades*, RWW

Sharky Water

As I write this, I am sitting at the helm of a forty-four-foot Thompson trawler, moored across the Sound, upriver from Tarpon Bay Marina, Sanibel Island, Florida, where I was once a fishing guide. It's late, nearly midnight. Beyond the frail incandescence of this wheelhouse is a van Gogh seascape: swirling stars and corridors of light on moving water. I can feel tide beneath the hull; can hear it currenting around pilings, drawn by a vacant moon. During my fishing-guide years—a time when many of the stories in this book were written—we would have described similar water as "sharky." To be sharky, water must be sufficiently dark and volatile to attract predators. It must demonstrate the potential to shield that which is unknown and may be dangerous. I like the idea that water flowing beneath this boat may well travel downriver, across Pine Island Sound, and end up in Tarpon Bay. I love the possibility that water once in Tarpon Bay—water upon which I fished—is, after several years of tidal influence, now moving among the mangrove feeder creeks of places I've been: Havana Harbor or the Chagres River in Panama, or up the San Juan into one of the most remote places on earth, Lake Nicaragua. I also love the image of sharks, sharks inhabiting some far-off sea place, cruising water that was once home to me and my marina buddies at Tarpon Bay. There are no gates out there. More than one of my old clients heard me say that, and it's true. No gates, you bet. All coastal places are more intimately linked to the wider world because of their connection to the sea. Ironically, though, it wasn't until I'd traveled the wider world that I began to understand that, as predators go, sharks do not compare to the dark creatures of our own construction . . .

There are a lot of sharky places out there. There're a lot of dark things cruising.

—*The Sharks of Lake Nicaragua,* RWW

Reef shark

Grilled Shark of Lake Nicaragua

When fishing for shark, the key is staying small. The bigger the shark, the tougher the meat. I eat anything under 5 feet. Once you have landed your meal, it is very important to bleed and ice your catch. A shark's blood contains urea, which is used to maintain body temperature. Once the shark dies, bacteria begins to break down the urea, converting it to ammonia, which will give the meat a sour taste. You can bleed the shark by making deep slits on either side of the tail base and then gutting it. Once the shark has been bled, put it on ice immediately. Steaking the shark is simple. Lay the shark on its stomach or side. Cut downward to the spine. The cartilage can be cut out or left in. The steaks should not be more than 1 inch in thickness. Both the skin and the spine, left in, are easily removed once cooked. —RWW

4 shark steaks, cut 1 inch thick

2 tablespoons butter

1 teaspoon pepper

½ teaspoon garlic salt

juice from 1 lime

1 lime, cut in wedges

Light coals for a medium to large grill or set heat to medium-high on a propane grill. Rub butter on both sides of shark steaks. Season steaks with pepper, garlic salt, and lime juice. Place on hot grill and cook 5 to 6 minutes on each side, or until steaks become firm and centers are white in color when tested with a fork. Serve garnished with lime wedges.

SERVES 4.

Recipe courtesy of Randy Wayne White.

This shark soon became shark steaks.

Fishing Sharks from a Kayak

Why fish for sharks from a kayak? I can't think of a single good reason. But isn't that one of the great things about paddling? If it offers an excuse to get out on the water, even a bad reason is good enough to justify crazed behavior. Here's why I told myself I should catch a shark while in my kayak: My old house sits on the remains of a shell pyramid that was inhabited for more than a thousand years by the indigenous people of this coast, the Calusa. The Calusa were once the region's dominant tribe. They built shell pyramids, plazas, and elaborate canals. They founded a sophisticated society that supported an elite military and exacted tribute from towns of hundreds of kilometers away. The Calusa were expert hunters and fishermen—for them, catching sharks from their dugout canoes was commonplace.

I like that. I also like the fact that my two-seater kayak rests on its side at the edge of the mound, probably not far from where, for centuries, other canoes were towed to rest. I like the fact that, when I rake the black dirt in my garden, I find chunks of pottery—remnants of bowls used to feed fishermen who walked this mound centuries before me. I also enjoy the realization that, each time I take paddle in hand, there is a metaphorical linkage across ten centuries; a connection of which I am a very real part. Such things insinuate genetic memory.

—*An American Traveler,* "Sharks from a Kayak," RWW

Terry Brennen, Carlene's husband, kayaking at sunset

Grilled Marinated Shark Fillets

Small black tip sharks, plentiful in the bay, were always a favorite grilled fish at Tarpon Bay Marina celebrations. —RWW

Garlic Butter:

1 pound butter, melted

¼ cup minced garlic

¼ cup minced shallots

¼ cup minced parsley

Teriyaki Marinade:

2 cups soy sauce

½ cup ginger brandy

1 cup hot water

½ pound brown sugar

½ cup honey

2 cups chilled canola oil

6 (8-ounce) shark fillets

For the garlic butter:

Place melted butter, garlic, shallots, and parsley in a medium bowl. Stir to mix ingredients. Set aside.

For the teriyaki marinade:

Place soy sauce, ginger brandy, water, brown sugar, and honey in the bowl of an electric mixer. Beat until smooth. With mixer on low speed, slowly add oil so that the mixture thickens.

For the shark fillets:

Place fillets in a covered container or zipper bag and cover with marinade of choice. Refrigerate and marinate overnight.

Preheat grill to medium-high. Place fillets on hot grill and cook 3 to 4 minutes. Turn fillets and brush with marinade or garlic butter. Cook 3 to 4 minutes more or until fillets are opaque and flake when tested with a fork.

SERVES 6.

Recipe courtesy of Timbers Restaurant & Fish Market on Sanibel.

In Search of Sharks

For three days I fished hard from my kayak; couldn't find a shark. Last night, looking for nothing but stars, I paddled out at midnight and a shark found me. A big one, too. It kept circling, nosing up to the thin fiberglass skin that separated me from the realities of saltwater. Can a 200-pound man hide in a kayak? Nope, but he can try.

I live near Sanibel Island off Florida's southwest coast. Estuaries here are a broth of single-celled plankton that glows when disturbed—a chemical interaction called bioluminescence. On the dark of the moon, with the tide just right, piffle strokes create swirling comet's tails. Fish streak away with the trajectory of meteorites. The path of every moving creature is illustrated by its own glittering contrail, which is how I knew that something big was approaching.

I was in waist-deep water when I saw a phosphorescent mass in the distance. It throbbed dull green, then bright green in serpentine rhythm. I watched it drawing closer as if vectoring toward some target, and then I realized that the target was me. Such realizations touch a primitive cord. It causes the nostrils to flare and the heart to shunt blood as the limbic brain assumes direct communication with the eager feet. Running, however, is an unsatisfactory option when a couple of miles from shore in a kayak. Not that I didn't give it some thought.

I stopped paddling. Silence is a sophisticated form of flight. Cowards and possums both think it is true. I listened to my own heartbeat, my own careful breathing as a shark, silhouetted in glittering green light, cruised slowly past. The creature was wider than my kayak, more than half as long. See a shark that large and you correctly think of it as an animal, not simply as a "fish." This animal was on the prowl. It was aware of movement. The life was mine.

I am not a romantic when it comes to sharks, nor am I prone to panic when around them. For thirteen years, I was a saltwater fishing guide at Sanibel's Tarpon Bay Marina. For some of those years, I tagged sharks for the National Marine Fisheries Services. I've handled hundreds of the things—enough to know that they are not sinister, nor scheming, nor deceptive, nor evil. Indeed, they are complex, sensitive creatures. Hollywood is prone to exaggeration. Some shock, huh? Had my encounter been staged for film, the shark would have torpedoed me out of the kayak, waited for the appropriate close-up, then demoted me to a very low rung on the food ladder. Instead, the animal cruised by a final time, close enough to touch. Then it vanished into its own world, the rhythm of its caudal fin lucent and steady as a heartbeat.

—An American Traveler, "Sharks from a Kayak," RWW

Flounder Baked in Spicy Tomato Sauce

Flounder is a delicious, mild-tasting fish and was considered a bonus when my charters caught one aboard my boat. —RWW

1 tablespoon olive oil

¾ cup chopped onions

2 cloves garlic, minced

1 tablespoon cornstarch

1 (16-ounce) can diced tomatoes, juice reserved

⅓ cup sliced stuffed green olives

1 teaspoon chopped red or green chili peppers

vegetable cooking spray

1½ pounds flounder fillets

salt to taste

1 tablespoon fresh lemon juice

Preheat oven to 375°F. Place olive oil in a medium skillet over medium heat. Add onions and garlic and cook until onions are translucent. Stir in cornstarch. Add tomatoes and their juices and stir until ingredients are well combined. Cook, stirring occasionally, until sauce thickens. Stir in olives and chili peppers.

Coat a 13 x 9-inch baking dish with vegetable cooking spray. Spoon half the sauce into the dish. Place fillets in a single layer over the sauce. Season with salt to taste and sprinkle with lemon juice. Top with remaining sauce and bake for 10 minutes, uncovered, or until fish flakes when tested with a fork.

SERVES 4.

Recipe courtesy of Lynda Leonard-Boyce.

"Flats" has become a generic saltwater term to describe a topography of bottom that is only a few feet below sea level. Typically, a flat is guttered with creeks and potholes, alive with sea grasses, corals, and sponges, and always affected by the wash of tides. —*Sharks from a Kayak*, RWW

Banana Leaf Snapper with Lime Cilantro Sauce

When I first met Chef Greg Nelson, I was impressed by his passion for food and fishing, and his talent for both. —RWW

Lime Cilantro Sauce:

½ cup dry-toasted sunflower seeds

10 whole garlic cloves

1 cup Parmesan cheese

½ cup fresh lime juice

salt and pepper

3 roasted jalapeños

1 cup canola oil

4 bunches cilantro, leaves removed

Snapper:

2 young banana leaves, blanched

⅛ cup ancho chili puree

¾ cup corn flour (masa)

1 tablespoon canola oil

warm water

salt and pepper

2 medium snapper fillets

¼ cup lime cilantro sauce

For the sauce:

Place sunflower seeds, garlic, cheese, lime juice, salt, pepper, and roasted jalapeños (which have been grilled until skin shrivels, then seeded and diced) in a blender. Puree until smooth. With blender running, slowly add 1 cup canola oil. When sauce has emulsified, add cilantro leaves and pulse a couple of times to chop leaves. Place sauce in a covered container and refrigerate until needed. Makes 1 cup.

For the snapper:

Preheat oven to 450°F. Cut a 12-inch square from each banana leaf. Spread ancho puree on center of leaf. Place masa in a small bowl and mix with 1 tablespoon oil and enough warm water to form a paste. Season with salt and pepper to taste. Place masa paste on ancho puree. Then place snapper fillets atop masa. Season with salt and pepper to taste. Fold in right and left sides of banana leaf. Then fold upper and lower sides, forming an envelope shape. Place stuffed banana leaf, folded side down, in a pie pan.

Add water to the pan, almost to top of snapper. Cover with another pie pan, inverted. Bake for 20 minutes. Meanwhile, place lime cilantro sauce in a small saucepan over medium-low heat and simmer until it is heated through.

Cut a large X in the top of the banana-leaf package and drizzle snapper with lime cilantro sauce. Serve with your favorite black beans and rice recipe.

SERVES 2.

Recipe courtesy of Chef Greg Nelson, Doc Ford's Sanibel Rum Bar & Grill.

The barrier islands of Florida's west coast have their own odor, their own feel. It's a fabric of strata and weight: seawater, sulfur muck, white sand, Gulf Stream allusions, and a wind that blows salt-heavy out of the Yucatan and Cuba. Think about hot coconut oil. Add a few drops of lime, then a drop or two of iodine. Dilute it with icebergs melted by ocean current; even if you've never been to Florida, reconstitute that mixture and you will know how the air feels and smells on the mangrove coast. —*The Mangrove Coast*, RWW

Captain Gene's Mullet

Gene Hamilton represents a fourth generation of Key West fishermen. His family has fished everywhere through the Everglades, and from the Keys to Cuba and back. There's even a lake in the Everglades named for one of his grandfathers. Gene, whose life would fill the pages of several books, used to rake Ernest Hemingway's yard in Key West as a boy. Once, while fishing for mullet along Bunche Beach, a panther came down and tried to steal his fish, tearing up his nets. As recently as the '90s, Captain Gene caught 12,000 pounds of mullet in one night, single-handedly! The net bans retired him from commercial fishing.

   2 mullets, filleted

   salt and pepper

   1 tablespoon canola oil

   1 onion, chopped

   2 servings instant grits

Season mullet fillets with salt and pepper to taste. Place canola oil in a large nonstick skillet over medium-high heat. Add fillets and onion to skillet. Sauté for 3 minutes. Gently turn fillets over and cook for 2 more minutes.

Meanwhile, cook grits per package instructions. Place grits on 2 dinner plates. Top each serving with half the mullet fillets and onions.

SERVES 2.

Recipe courtesy of Gene Hamilton and K. S. Young and A. L. Rainey of *A Back Bay Look at Culinary Delights.*

Gene Hamilton was a man admired by many. We lost him in 2012. I would like to think he is in heaven swapping stories about Key West with Ernest Hemingway or keeping company with fishing great Billy Pate. Now there was someone who could tell a good fish story. We will miss them all. —RWW

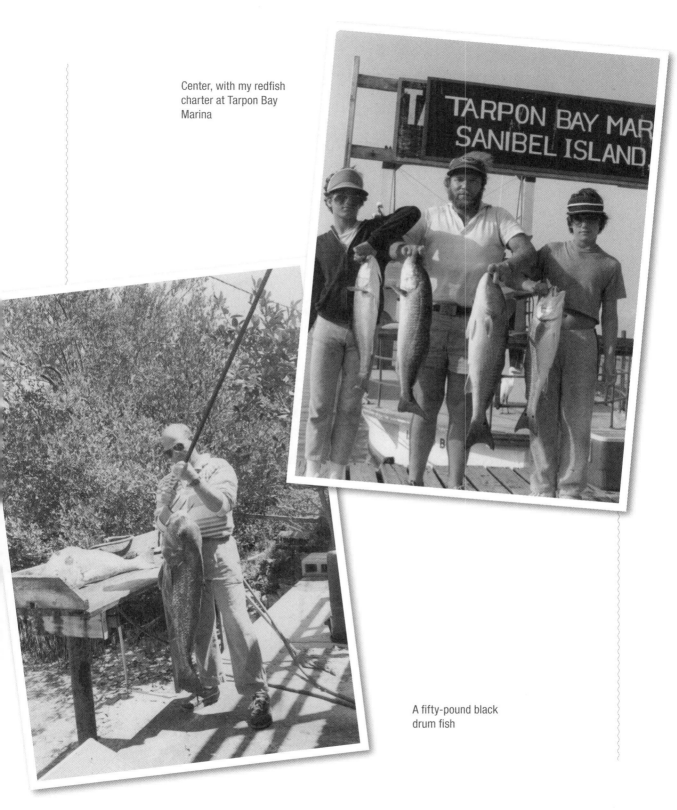

Center, with my redfish charter at Tarpon Bay Marina

A fifty-pound black drum fish

Pan-Seared Pompano with Summer Marinara Sauce

Once again, Captain Matt Mitchell works his magic with this marvelous fish dish. —RWW

¼ cup extra virgin olive oil

1 large red onion, diced

6 large garlic cloves, chopped

1 bunch Italian parsley, chopped

2 bunches fresh basil, chopped

½ bunch fresh oregano, chopped

3 pounds plum tomatoes, cut into small pieces

4 cooked artichoke hearts, sliced

1 (11-ounce) jar kalamata olives, drained, seeded, and chopped

1 (3½-ounce) jar capers, drained

1 pound dried penne or other small tubular pasta

6 pompano fillets, skin scored

sea salt and pepper

1 lemon, cut into 6 wedges

1½ cups Parmesan Reggiano cheese

Place 2 tablespoons olive oil in a large skillet over medium-high heat. When oil is almost smoking, add onion, garlic, parsley, basil, and oregano. Sauté, stirring constantly, until garlic starts to brown (but be careful it doesn't burn). Remove skillet from heat and add tomatoes, artichoke hearts, olives, and capers. Set aside.

Cook pasta in a large pot of boiling water per package instructions. Drain pasta and toss with marinara sauce.

Meanwhile, season pompano fillets with salt and pepper to taste. Place another large skillet over medium heat. Add 2 tablespoons olive oil to skillet. When oil is hot, add fillets to skillet, flesh side down. Sear for 1 minute. Gently turn fillets over and continue cooking 3 to 4 minutes or until fish flakes when tested with a fork.

To serve: Place a generous serving of pasta on each of 6 dinner plates. Top each with a pompano fillet. Garnish each with a lemon wedge and serve with freshly grated Parmesan Reggiano cheese.

SERVES 6.

Recipe courtesy of Captain Matt Mitchell, St. James City, Florida.

Holding my world-record crevalle jack at
Tarpon Bay Marina. We definitely celebrated
with a few beers that day. —RWW

Sanibel Marina

Grouper Dijon

The fish don't get much fresher than at Gramma Dot's, located at Sanibel Marina. I've always admired the guides there. —RWW

2 tablespoons Dijon mustard

¼ cup white wine

1 tablespoon lemon juice

dried dill weed

2 tablespoons butter, melted

vegetable cooking spray

1 pound grouper fillets, cut ½ inch thick

Preheat oven to 450°F. Place mustard, wine, lemon juice, 2 pinches dill weed, and melted butter in a small bowl. Whisk to combine ingredients.

Coat an 11 x 7-inch baking dish with vegetable cooking spray. Place grouper fillets in a single layer in dish. Spread mustard sauce over fillets. Bake for 5 minutes or until fish flakes when tested with a fork.

SERVES 2.

Recipe courtesy of Gramma Dot's at the Sanibel Marina on Sanibel Island.

Marina manager Graeme displays
a nice size tripletail

The Twig Syndrome

I had celebrated my 1,800th career fishing charter by attending taco night at a bar on Sanibel Island, and before leaving for Costa Rica, had guided more than a hundred trips during a four-month period, a withering schedule of being on the docks before light and finishing at the cleaning table just before dark. It is this marathon of wind and water, plus the Florida tourist rush, that produces in the operators of fishing vessels a phenomenon known as Twig Syndrome, or Guides' Disease, a psychological distemper with a whole bunch of unattractive symptoms: Snapping like a dry twig is one, and maybe leaving your boat to go on a fishing vacation is another.

—*The Best of Outside Magazine,* "The Twig Syndrome," RWW

Aboard my boat

CHAPTER 12

MEAT AND POULTRY

Rising out of the saw grass were dome islands
of cypress trees, from which snowy egrets flushed:
long-necked birds blooming from the shadows
like bright white flowers. There were tarpon rolling
at the mouth of the river and, farther up, alligators
the color of raw pottery, baking on mud slicks.

—*The Heat Islands,* RWW

Bailey Track,
J. N. "Ding" Darling
National Wildlife
Refuge at sunset

~ 149

Beef

Marinated Beef Strips

Beef marinated on a stick (in a very similar version of this delicious snack) is cooked on a small wood or charcoal-fired grill, on street corners in many countries and islands throughout the tropics. Singapore comes to mind, and Raffels Hotel. —RWW

½ pound sirloin steak or beef roast

1 small onion

¾ teaspoon salt

pepper

1½ tablespoons lemon juice

1 cup sour cream

lettuce

lemon wedges

Cut cooked sirloin steak or beef roast into thin strips. Thinly slice onion; separate into rings. Combine beef, onion, salt, and dash of pepper. Sprinkle with lemon juice. Stir in dairy sour cream. Chill. Serve in lettuce-lined dishes with lemon wedges.

MAKES 6 SERVINGS.

Recipe courtesy of Randy Wayne White.

In the strange storm light, coconut palms leaning in feathered strands are isolated, set apart from the mangrove beach where they grow. They appear fragile and singular, gold and green, as if shaped by a hurricane wind, then marooned in stillness.

—*Tarpon Fishing in Mexico and Florida*, RWW

Tournedos Chasseur

The Old Captiva House at 'Tween Waters Inn on Captiva Island is an enchanting restaurant situated between the Gulf of Mexico and Bay waters. A popular honeymoon destination known for romantic dinners and beautiful sunsets. —RWW

4 (4-ounce) petite beef filets

2 teaspoons cracked pepper

2 tablespoons canola oil, divided

½ cup wild mushrooms, such as shiitakes or oyster, cleaned and sliced

4 plum tomatoes, peeled, seeded, and finely chopped

6 whole garlic cloves, roasted

¼ cup red wine

2 teaspoons Worcestershire sauce

6 ounces veal glace

2 slices white bread

Season both sides of the four filets with cracked pepper. Place 1 tablespoon canola oil in a large nonstick skillet over medium-high heat. When oil is hot, add filets and sear for 1 minute. Turn steaks and sear other side for 1 minute or until steaks are medium-rare. Place steaks on a platter and cover with aluminum foil to keep them warm.

Add 1 tablespoon canola oil to hot skillet. Add mushrooms, tomatoes, and roasted garlic and sauté, stirring occasionally, until mushrooms are cooked through, about 5 minutes. Reduce heat to medium-low. Add red wine and Worcestershire sauce and stir to combine. Stir in veal glace and cook, stirring occasionally, until sauce is thickened.

Meanwhile, make toast points. Trim crusts from bread. Place bread in toaster and toast on light setting. Cut toast in half on the diagonal, twice, to form 4 triangles.

Arrange 4 toast points on each of 2 dinner plates. Top each plate with 2 filet mignons. Top steaks with sauce.

SERVES 2.

Recipe courtesy of The Old Captiva House at 'Tween Waters Inn on Captiva Island.

Ribs Jamaican

I don't like Jamaica, probably the nastiest airport officials on Earth, but you can't go wrong with this recipe from The Lazy Flamingo. —RWW

4 pounds of baby back ribs

1 tablespoon seasoned salt

1 teaspoon Jamaican jerk spice

Preheat oven to 375°F. Place ribs in a roasting pan. (Be sure pan is deep enough to allow ribs to be covered by water.) Sprinkle ribs with seasoned salt and jerk spice. Cover ribs with water, then cover pan with lid or aluminum foil. Cook until ribs are fork-tender, about 45 minutes.

SERVES 2.

Recipe courtesy of The Lazy Flamingo, in two locations on Sanibel Island.

Dock lights shimmered, strips of gold on liquid darkness, funneling out across the bay. Most of the boats were lighted too, sitting in rows looking bright and Christmasy, vibrating with muted laughter, wild sentence fragments rising above night sound. —*Sanibel Flats*, RWW

Steak 'n' Mushroom Kabobs

Cooking over hot coals may seem primitive to some, but for me, it brings back fond memories of when my sons were growing up. —RWW

½ cup red wine

½ cup canola oil

1 clove garlic, minced

½ teaspoon dried basil

1 teaspoon salt

2 tablespoons ketchup

1 tablespoon Worcestershire sauce

2 to 2½ pounds sirloin steak, cut into 2-inch cubes

8 ounces large button mushrooms, cleaned, with stems removed

Place wine, oil, garlic, basil, salt, ketchup, and Worcestershire sauce in a medium bowl and whisk to combine. Place steak and mushrooms in a large, freezer-weight zipper bag. Add marinade to zipper bag. Close zipper and shake to coat steaks and mushrooms with marinade. Refrigerate overnight.

Preheat grill. Drain steak and mushrooms in a colander. Thread steak and mushrooms on metal skewers. (If using wooden skewers, soak them in warm water for 30 minutes before using.) Place skewers on grill, turning occasionally, until steak is medium-rare when tested with a knife. (If you wish the steak to be well-done, thread meat and mushrooms on separate skewers so that mushrooms don't overcook. If you prefer to grill kabobs over hot coals, turn occasionally until desired degree of doneness.)

SERVES 6.

Recipe courtesy of Jerry's of Sanibel Island.

Cabbage Key Cheeseburger in Paradise

Cabbage Key, owned by my dear friends Rob and Phyllis Wells, is a Florida classic, historically and in the culinary arts. The restaurant there has elevated the cheeseburger to art form—and I love the potato salad, too. In the 1970s, Capt. Jimmy Buffett spent time there. The man is a brilliant lyricist, and his "Cheeseburger in Paradise" is also a classic—which may be why nearly every island in the Keys and Caribbean claims he wrote the song there. I don't know the truth but I do know the burgers at Cabbage Key are memorable.

Cabbage Key uses only certified Angus ground beef that has never been frozen. Each 7-ounce patty is 2 inches thick. Chefs cook each burger on a flame grill to sear them, and then they cook the meat on a flat-top grill to medium-well. Each hot burger is topped with American cheese and presented in a fresh sesame-seed bun. Accompanied by ripe Florida tomatoes, fresh lettuce and onions, and mayonnaise on the side, the Cabbage Key creation truly ranks as a cheeseburger in paradise. The island on which this marvelous historic establishment sits is only a short boat drive from my house on Pineland.—RWW

28 ounces certified Angus ground beef

4 sesame-seed buns

4 thick tomato slices

4 slices onion

4 iceberg lettuce leaves

½ cup mayonnaise

Form ground beef into four 7-ounce patties that are 2 inches thick. Preheat gas grill to high. Place patties on grill and sear each side. Reduce heat to medium and continue cooking until patties are cooked to your temperature of choice.

Place each burger in a sesame-seed bun. Top each with a slice of tomato, onion, and a lettuce leaf. Serve with mayonnaise on the side.

SERVES 4.

Recipe courtesy of Cabbage Key.

Carlene interviewed Jimmy Buffett on Sanibel in 1984 when he was promoting his new T-shirt line. The cookbook would not be complete without a recipe of this very popular Florida staple.

At sunrise, the sun burned through a glowing curtain of peach and rust. At sunset, the sand-laced eastern sky caught the light and reflected desert gold. At night, the clouds smoldered in the wind and throbbed with dull flame. . . . There was television, Nintendo, tourist traffic, air-conditioned malls, lottery tickets, Epcot, condo association meetings, greyhound races, cool, dark bars, and water beds. October in Florida is hot. People don't get out to look at the sky much. —*The Man Who Invented Florida*, RWW

Sunset over Sanibel Island

Smoked and Cured Meats

Salt-Curing Meat in Brine

Curing meat by using a salt brine was a widely used method of preserving meat before the days of refrigeration. Many parts of the tropics are still without electricity, let alone refrigeration. Always ask to look at the meat before ordering. Don't worry, the cook will not be insulted, but will regard you as a savvy traveler.

Fill a bucket or brine barrel and let meat soak for 6 days. Now that your meat is salted, remove the meat from the brine, dry it off, and put it in flour- or gunnysacks to keep the flies away. Then, hang it up in a cool dry place. If it goes bad, you'll know it!

For Longer Keeping:

Fill a brine barrel, halfway, with 4 cups brown sugar to 3 gallons of water and 1 cup of vinegar. (Note: No salt.) Inject some of the sugar brine mixture into the already salted meat with a syringe, if available, and then put the meat in the sugar brine for 3 days.

Remove the meat from the brine and smoke it for three days. Now, put your smoked meat into flour- or gunnysacks to keep the flies away, and hang it up in a cool, dry place to store. —RWW

Blustery night with winter stars. Not quite cold enough for breath to condense, but cold enough to shock the skin and maybe help quiet my brain. I stood on the porch looking out across the bay. Watched mullet stir green arcs through the water; heard a night heron squawk. Listened to waves slap at the pilings of my house—a boat-hull sound without rhythm, without order. —*North of Havana*, RWW

Brine-Cured Pork

8 pounds salt (Note: 1 part salt to 48 parts water)

2 pounds raw sugar or brown sugar

2 ounces saltpeter

5 gallons water

100 pounds pork

Mix salt, brown sugar, and saltpeter, add this to the water, and bring the mixture to a boil. Stir to dissolve sugar. Skim off any scum that may form while boiling after everything is dissolved. Remove from heat and chill. Let it cool.

Pack the pieces of meat into clean barrels or earthenware crocks, placing them as close together as possible. Now pour the cold brine over the meat, making absolutely certain that the meat is completely covered. Put a board over the meat that just fits inside the container, and place weights on it to make sure that the meat is submerged in the brine. When curing larger and smaller pieces of meat at the same time, place the larger pieces on the bottom and the smaller ones on top. This is so the smaller ones can be lifted out without disturbing the larger pieces. The small pieces do not take as long to cure as the bigger ones.

When the meat is cured in warm temperatures, the brine may show signs of souring. If this should happen, remove the meat and soak it in lukewarm water for an hour or so. Wash the meat in fresh cold water and throw out the soured brine. Clean out the container, repack the meat, and make a fresh brine in original proportions.

Bacon sides and loins require 2 days per pound in the brine. Shoulders will take 3 days per pound. Hams will take 4 days per pound.

After the meat is cured, the pieces should be soaked in warm water and then washed in cool water or even scrubbed with a brush to remove any scum that may have accumulated during the curing process.

Hang the meat by very heavy cords in a smokehouse and allow to drain 24 hours before starting the smoking.

Oak wood is the best to use for smoking, and the temperature in the smokehouse should be 100 to 120°F. The ventilators should be left open at first to allow any moisture to escape. Smoke until desired flavor and color is arrived at.

Nick and I discuss the day's catch.

All marinas are more than a sum total of docks and property, bait wells, ships' stores, and receipts. They are communities; ephemeral colonies with personalities as varied as the individuals who form them. —*Sanibel Flats*, RWW

Red mangrove forest at J. N. "Ding" Darling National Wildlife Refuge (Red Mangrove Overlook)

Poultry

Georgia Wilson White's North Carolina Fried Chicken

The delightful smell of fried chicken cooking on the stove brings back wonderful memories of my mother in the kitchen. This is my mother's recipe. —RWW

Two slices of salt pork

2 eggs

2 cups buttermilk

3 pounds chicken pieces

2 cups flour

2 teaspoons coarsely ground
   black pepper

½ cup lard or shortening

Georgia Wilson White

At low heat, render salt pork in large frying pan.

Crack eggs into buttermilk. Soak chicken in egg-buttermilk mixture for 15 minutes. Combine flour and pepper. Coat chicken well with mixture. Remove salt pork from frying pan, and add lard or shortening. Heat oil in pan on high medium heat. Add chicken. Reduce heat to medium. Cover and cook 15 minutes on 1 side, turn and cook covered on medium heat until tender and brown (about 20 minutes).

SERVES 4 TO 6.

Recipe courtesy of Randy Wayne White.

Memories of home—the Sanibel
Historical Village and Museum

Apple Cranberry Casserole

Looking for another way to cook cranberries? This marvelous recipe from my Aunt Johnsie Wilson Russo may be your answer. This recipe goes with almost any poultry dish. Carlene already has it added to her Thanksgiving menu. —RWW

3 cups sliced Rome apples (unpeeled)

2 cups raw cranberries or 2 cups frozen cranberries, defrosted

½ cup sugar

1 stick butter (or margarine)

⅓ cup self-rising flour

½ cup light brown sugar

½ cup pecans, chopped (optional)

Line 9 x11-inch greased casserole dish with apples and cranberries. In pan melt 1 stick butter, ⅓ cup flour, light brown sugar, and ½ cup chopped pecans (optional). Mix well. Spread mixture over apples and cranberries. Bake (uncovered) 40–45 minutes at 350°F.

SERVES 6.

Recipe courtesy of Randy Wayne White.

Johnsie Wilson Russo

It was sunset, the pearly after time, and the sky over Sanibel Island was wind-streaked with cantaloupe orange, purple swirls of cloud. Beyond the docks, mangroves settled charcoal black, blurring into smoky hedges as light drained from the bay. —*The Man Who Invented Florida*, RWW

I meet such nice people at my book signings.

Curried Chicken

What a wonderful way to prepare chicken. —RWW

1 cup flour

4 (5-ounce) boneless chicken breasts, trimmed and pounded flat

¼ cup clarified butter

¼ teaspoon cumin

⅛ teaspoon minced fresh ginger

½ teaspoon minced garlic

¼ cup dry white wine

1 teaspoon curry powder

1 cup heavy cream

1 teaspoon raisins

Place flour on a dinner plate and dredge chicken breasts in flour. Place a large nonstick skillet over medium heat. Add butter. When butter is hot, add chicken. Sauté chicken until underside is golden brown, about 2 minutes. Turn chicken and sauté until other side is golden brown, about 1 minute more. Remove chicken breasts to a plate and cover with aluminum foil.

Add cumin, ginger, garlic, and wine to the skillet. Stir and cook until liquid has reduced by half. Add curry powder, cream, and raisins. Stir to combine. Reduce heat to medium-low. Add chicken breasts back to skillet. Cook until sauce has thickened. Serve over rice.

SERVES 4.

Recipe courtesy of The Jacaranda on Sanibel Island.

Mesquite Grilled Chicken with Herbed Wild Rice, Apples, and Walnuts

This was one of Carlene's favorite dishes at The Nutmeg House on Sanibel. A memory of the past. —RWW

1 (6-ounce) package wild rice mix

8 tablespoons butter, divided

2 garlic cloves, minced

½ bunch scallions, finely chopped

½ bunch fresh basil, finely chopped

½ bunch fresh mint, finely chopped

½ bunch fresh dill, finely chopped

½ bunch fresh chives, finely chopped

½ bunch fresh parsley, finely chopped

mesquite chips for the grill

6 boneless chicken breasts, lightly pounded

olive oil spray

2 large Granny Smith apples, cored and sliced

½ pound Havarti cheese, sliced

juice of 1 lemon

1 cup finely chopped walnuts

Prepare wild rice mix according to package instructions and set aside. Place 4 tablespoons butter in a large nonstick skillet over medium-low heat. When butter has melted, add garlic and sauté until aromatic. Add scallions and half of the basil, mint, dill, chives, and parsley. Add wild rice and stir to combine ingredients. Cook, stirring occasionally, until rice mixture is heated through. Turn off burner and cover skillet so that rice stays warm.

Add mesquite chips to grill and preheat. Coat chicken breasts with olive oil spray and place on grill. Grill chicken 3 minutes. Turn chicken and grill 3 minutes more or until chicken has just turned opaque in the center when tested with a knife.

Preheat broiler. Place rice mixture on a heatproof platter. Place grilled chicken breasts atop rice. Sprinkle apple slices and cheese atop chicken. Place under broiler until cheese has melted.

Meanwhile, melt remaining 4 tablespoons butter in a small skillet over low heat. Add lemon juice and remaining herbs and stir to mix. Spoon herbed lemon butter over cheese and rice. Sprinkle with chopped walnuts.

SERVES 6.

Chicken Romano

I'm always looking for a new chicken recipe. A marvelous combination of ingredients. —RWW

4 eggs, slightly beaten

½ cup grated Parmesan cheese

½ tablespoon chopped parsley

1 teaspoon minced garlic

¼ cup olive oil

4 boneless chicken breasts

Place eggs, Parmesan cheese, parsley, and garlic in a small bowl. Whisk to form a medium-thick batter. Set aside.

Place olive oil in a large skillet over medium heat. Dip chicken breasts into batter, coating evenly, and place in hot oil. Place battered chicken in hot oil and sauté until golden brown, about 4 minutes. Turn chicken and reduce heat to medium-low. Sauté 5 minutes or until chicken is just cooked through and no longer opaque when tested with a knife.

SERVES 4.

Recipe courtesy of The Normandie at the West Wind Inn on Sanibel Island.

I saw my first sea turtle; a huge green turtle flapping out of the murk. The animal was as big as me; it had to weigh more than two hundred pounds. Its carapace was olive hued and fouled with benthic travelers. The stroke of its flippers mimicked the wind stroke of seabirds; barnacles on its shell mimicked the shapes of spent volcanoes.

—*An Island Off Borneo*, RWW

Charcoal Grilled Duck with Raspberry Sauce

This was a popular dish at the Quarterdeck Restaurant on Sanibel. When the local establishment closed, residents and visitors alike missed the restaurant's local charm. —RWW

Duck:

1 (5-pound) duck

2 carrots, peeled and halved

1 medium onion, peeled and quartered

sprig of whole thyme

Raspberry Sauce:

1 (15-ounce) can raspberries

1 tablespoon crème de cassis

2 teaspoons white vinegar

2 tablespoons brown sugar

½ teaspoon soy sauce

¼ cup red wine

¼ cup white wine

¼ cup water

¼ cup cornstarch

Preheat oven to 400°F. Remove giblets and neck from duck and discard. Rinse duck cavity and dry with paper toweling. Place carrots and onion into cavity. Rub duck skin with whole thyme. Place duck in roasting pan. Place pan in oven and roast duck for 45 minutes.

While duck is roasting, prepare raspberry sauce. With the back of a spoon, force raspberries through a strainer, into a medium saucepan. Place saucepan over medium heat. Add crème de cassis, vinegar, brown sugar, soy sauce, and wines. Bring to a boil. Reduce heat to low. Mix water and cornstarch together in a small bowl. Add to raspberry mixture, whisking constantly until sauce has thickened. Turn off burner and cover saucepan.

Remove duck from oven and allow it to cool. When duck is cool, remove vegetables from cavity and discard. Cut duck in half and debone body cavity.

Preheat grill. Place duck halves on grill and cook until hot, crisp, and fork-tender. Test with an instant-read thermometer. Duck is done when internal temperature reaches 190°F. (Be careful that rendered duck fat does not flare flames.) Serve with warm raspberry sauce.

SERVES 2.

Recipe courtesy of The Lighthouse Café on Sanibel Island.

Windsurfing Pine Island Sound at sunset

Pork, Lamb, and Veal

Chasing the Pig

I first sensed the potential for trouble in Nicaragua about a year after the war, when I chased a pig up the steps of a cathedral toward the open doors of what might have been the sacred vestry. The pig was smart; a vestry was exactly the safe harbor he would have chosen. But participants in the wedding that had just ended were not amused, and who can blame them?

There they stood, men in Guayabera shirts, women in their finery, bride and groom, maids and ushers, spilling out over the banks of steps that led up to the stone basilica. Maybe they were throwing rice, maybe the bride was about to toss the bouquet, I can't say—I was attacking the pig. Then here we came, zigzagging through the wedding party, a squealing swine with a 215-pound gringo in hot pursuit, one perhaps headed for the sanctuary of the chapel, the other realizing, too late, headed for trouble.

This was in Grenada, Nicaragua's most beautiful city, where herding cloven-hoofed animals through cathedrals is generally discouraged. Grenada is an ancient municipality of cobbled streets, open markets, marble columns, and ornate parks, everything filmed by a layer of grime and the shadow of this Central American nation's withering poverty. But there is a nice Castilian light to the town; a cosmopolitan savvy not found anywhere else in the country. Grenada is located an hour southeast of Managua on the shore of Lake Nicaragua, the twentieth-largest lake in the world.

Rural Central America smells unlike anyplace I have ever been. Nearly all that there is to see can be found in the air as well as wood smoke from cooking fires, cattle pastures and fruit stands, diesel fumes of public buses, the saturated earth smells of jungle rivers. Here the land still makes itself known.

—*The Sharks of Lake Nicaragua*, RWW

Pan-Broiled Veal Chops

Chef David Wackerman's memorable meals included formal French and Northern Italian dishes. Veal was one of David's specialties. Wonderful dining memories from the past. —RWW

6 rib veal chops, cut 1 ½ inches thick—
about 12 ounces each

2 tablespoons olive oil

¼ cup dry white wine

1 medium onion, chopped

1 large celery rib, chopped

1 medium carrot, chopped

1 large bay leaf

1 medium garlic clove, chopped

1 teaspoon tomato paste

1 teaspoon salt

¼ teaspoon fresh ground pepper

6 cups water

2 tablespoons unsalted butter

Bone the chops and set the meat and bone on separate plates. In a large skillet, preferably cast iron, heat 1 tablespoon of the oil over high heat. When the oil is hot, add the veal bones and cook, turning occasionally until dark brown, about 12 minutes. Transfer with tongs to a plate.

Pour off grease in the pan. Add the wine and deglaze the pan by scraping any brown from the bottom with a wooden spoon. Return the browned bones to the pan and add the onion, celery, carrots, bay leaf, garlic, tomato paste, salt, and pepper. Add 6 cups of water and bring to a boil. Reduce the heat to low and simmer gently for 1 hour.

Remove the bones and discard. Pour the stock through a fine-mesh sieve into a medium saucepan. Let sit for 1 hour. Skim off the fat. Bring to a boil over high heat. Boil until it has reduced to one cup, about 30 minutes.

Heat a large heavy skillet, preferably cast iron, over high heat and add the remaining one tablespoon of oil. When the oil is hot, add the veal and cook about 3 minutes on each side, or until lightly browned. Reduce the heat to moderate and cook for 4 minutes on each side until lightly browned or medium pink inside. Transfer to a platter; cover to keep warm.

Place the reduced stock in the skillet over high heat. Boil for 4 minutes until reduced to ½ cup and then remove from heat. Pour in any exuded juice from the cooked meat. Whisk in the butter until incorporated.

Serve the veal chops on individual dinner plate over a pool of the sauce.

SERVES 6.

Brazilian Potato and Meat Pie

I first tasted this dish—called Nhoques de Forno (NYOH-kees day FOHR-noh)—in Peru on assignment for *Outside* magazine. I got stabbed there in Peru, not at the magazine. —RWW

8 medium potatoes, peeled and quartered

1 teaspoon salt

1 cup warm milk

2 tablespoons butter, melted

2 eggs, lightly beaten

½ cup mild cheddar cheese, grated

3 tablespoons cornstarch

3 tablespoons flour

½ teaspoon salt

vegetable cooking spray

½ pound thinly sliced ham

½ pound thinly sliced mozzarella cheese

Any day is a good day on the water.

Place potatoes and salt in a large saucepan with water to cover. Bring water to boil over medium-high heat. Reduce heat to medium-low and cook until potatoes are cooked through and soft. Drain potatoes in a colander.

Place potatoes in the bowl of an electric mixer. Add warm milk, melted butter, eggs, cheddar cheese, cornstarch, flour, and salt. Mix on low speed until smooth.

Preheat oven to 300°F. Coat a 9 x 13-inch baking dish with vegetable cooking spray. Spread half of the potato mixture in dish. Top with ham slices, then mozzarella. Spread remaining potato mixture on top and bake for 30 minutes. Remove from oven.

SERVES 6.

Recipe courtesy of Randy Wayne White.

Breaded Pork Tenderloin Sandwich

Once served at The Snooty Fox on Sanibel, which was a fun place. But this tasty dish can still be found at the Sanibel Café. —RWW

1 (24-ounce) pork tenderloin cut into 4 (6-ounce) pieces

2 cups milk

1 egg, lightly beaten

1 cup flour

1 cup cracker crumbs

canola oil

Using a sharp knife, butterfly tenderloin pieces, cutting almost in half. Place pieces between two layers of wax paper and pound until about 6 inches in diameter.

Mix milk and egg together in a medium bowl. Mix flour and cracker crumbs together on a dinner plate. Dip tenderloin pieces in milk-egg wash and then into flour-crumb mix, patting to cover entire piece of meat.

Place a large skillet over medium-high heat. Add canola oil to measure 1 inch up the side of the skillet. Bring oil to 350°F. Fry tenderloin pieces for about 5 minutes, turning once, or until pork is golden brown. Serve on fresh kaiser rolls.

SERVES 4.

Talking to marina guide
Captain Alex Payne

To the west, only a few degrees above the horizon, the sun was the smoky orange of a hunter's moon. Because it was precisely bisected by a band of purple stratus clouds, there was a ringed effect—as if Saturn were ablaze and spinning on a collision course toward Earth. The harsh light flattened itself across the prairie, horizon to horizon, turning feathered saw grass to gold, turning the mushroom shapes of distant cypress heads to silver. —*Everglades*, RWW

Visitors enjoyed shelling, nature tours, and back-bay fishing aboard the *Island Belle*, docked at Tarpon Bay marina.

Rack of Lamb

Lamb dishes at the charming Captiva Inn were a diner's delight. A memory from the past. —RWW

2 racks of lamb (8 bones each), trimmed, frenched, and with chine bone removed

salt and pepper

6 tablespoons oil

2 cloves garlic, minced

½ cup white wine

1 tablespoon mint jelly

2 tablespoons plus ½ cup Dijon mustard

1 cup heavy cream

1 cup fresh bread crumbs

1 sprig fresh rosemary, leaves removed

Preheat oven to 400°F. Season each rack with salt and pepper to taste. Place oil in a large nonstick skillet over high heat. When oil is hot, quickly sear the lamb on all exposed sides. Remove racks, set aside, and allow to cool.

Place garlic in a medium saucepan over high heat. Add white wine and cook until wine is reduced by about one-third. Add mint jelly and 2 tablespoons mustard and cook for 3 minutes, stirring frequently. Reduce heat to medium. Add heavy cream and reduce sauce for five minutes, stirring constantly.

Meanwhile, using a brush, baste lamb racks lightly with ½ cup mustard, covering all except the bones. Place bread crumbs on a dinner plate. Dredge each rack in crumbs to coat and place on a rimmed baking sheet. Sprinkle fresh rosemary leaves on the lamb. Place baking sheet in oven and bake lamb 15 minutes for rare, 20 minutes for medium-rare, and 25 minutes for well-done. Cut racks between bones. Place a pool of sauce on each of 4 dinner plates. Fan half a rack of lamb (4 chops) atop each pool of sauce.

SERVES 4.

Sea-oats on Bowman's Beach,
Sanibel Island

CHAPTER 13

VEGETABLES, POTATOES, BEANS, AND RICE

Pine Island Sound more closely resembled a flooded golf course than a saltwater estuary. The bar was exposed, dry and firm, a temporary peninsula ten meters wide and several miles long. On the Sanibel side, separated by a fringe of muck, were red mangroves elevated above the water on monkey-bar roots. On the bay side were hundreds of acres of turtle grass as green as spring wheat, that plateau of green pocked with sea pools and guttered by creeks. —*Shark River*, RWW

Vegetables

Grilled Italian Vegetables

A simple but tasty dish from Carlene's friend Lynda, this side dish is easy to prepare on the grill. Grilling is one of my favorite ways to cook. —RWW

vegetable cooking spray

3 medium zucchini squash, cut into ¼-inch-thick angled slices

1 medium onion, thinly sliced

2 medium tomatoes, cored and quartered

salt and pepper

sweet basil leaves, finely chopped

4 teaspoons butter, cut into small pieces

Preheat grill. Coat bottom of an aluminum foil pan with vegetable cooking spray. Place zucchini in center, top with onions, and arrange tomatoes around the perimeter of the zucchini. Season with salt, pepper, and basil to taste. Dot with butter. Cover pan tightly with aluminum foil. Grill for 30 to 35 minutes.

SERVES 4.

Recipe courtesy of Lynda Leonard-Boyce.

The mangrove is a rugged wind-stunted tree that elevates itself above swamp on monkey-bar roots. Because the tree employs its arched roots to creep and expand, it is called the "tree that walks," the name itself alluding to qualities of silence that hint at dark groves of speechless men. —*The Mangrove Coast*, RWW

Great egrets in black
mangrove forest

Broccoli Soufflé

Another popular dish from Calamity Jane's on Sanibel, a short distance from the marina. A memory from the past. —RWW

    3 tablespoons butter

    3 tablespoons flour

    1 teaspoon salt

    1 cup milk

    ¼ teaspoon nutmeg

    1 tablespoon lemon juice

    2 bunches fresh broccoli, cooked, drained, and chopped

    4 egg yolks, beaten

    4 egg whites, beaten until stiff

    vegetable cooking spray

Preheat oven to 325°F. Place butter in a 4-quart saucepan over medium heat. When butter has melted, whisk in flour and salt until mixture bubbles. Slowly add milk, whisking until sauce is smooth and thick. Add nutmeg, lemon juice, and broccoli. Stir to combine.

Remove saucepan from heat and allow mixture to cool for about 15 minutes. Whisk in egg yolks. Allow mixture to cool another 15 minutes, then gently fold in the egg whites. Transfer broccoli mixture to a 1½-quart soufflé dish that has been coated with vegetable cooking spray. Place dish in a deep roasting pan. Add water to the pan so that it reaches one-third of the way up the side of the soufflé dish. Place soufflé, in its water bath, in oven and bake for 1 hour or until soufflé is set. Serve immediately.

SERVES 6.

Summer Squash Casserole

Most families have a favorite squash casserole recipe, especially if you are from the South. This recipe was given to Carlene by her ex-mother-in-law, Claire Baum, a wonderful Jewish cook. According to Carlene, she made even the most meager meal a delightful dining experience. —RWW

2 cups sliced yellow squash

1 small onion chopped

1 (16-ounce) carton sour cream

1 (10¾-ounce) can cream of mushroom soup

1 (14-ounce) package Pepperidge Farm Stuffing Mix

8 tablespoons melted butter or margarine

Preheat oven to 350°F. Place squash in a medium saucepan with water to cover. Bring to a boil over medium-high heat. Reduce heat to medium and cook until squash are fork-tender. Drain squash. Refresh with cold water and drain again.

Place squash and onion in a large bowl. Toss to mix ingredients. Place sour cream and soup in a small bowl. Stir to mix, then add mixture to vegetables. Toss until vegetables are well coated. Place stuffing mix in a large bowl. Add melted butter and stir with a fork until stuffing is well coated with butter. Add stuffing to vegetable mixture and toss well to combine ingredients. Bake, uncovered in a shallow baking dish, for 35 to 40 minutes.

SERVES 4 TO 6.

Recipe courtesy of Carlene Fredericka Brennen.

Broccoli Casserole

If my dear Aunt Della Wilson Denson listed crackers in her recipes it was usually Ritz. I think most kids grew up with a taste for those buttery favorites. —RWW

2 (10-ounce) packages of broccoli, frozen

1(10¾ ounce) can cream of mushroom soup

1 cup mayonnaise

2 eggs, beaten

¼ cup onion, chopped

1 teaspoon salt

1 teaspoon pepper

1¾ cup grated extra sharp cheddar cheese

1 cup cracker crumbs

½ stick margarine, melted

Cook broccoli and drain. Mix all ingredients except 1 cup of grated cheese, cracker crumbs and margarine. Put in 13 x 9-inch casserole dish. Mix margarine with cracker crumbs. Sprinkle remaining cheese and cracker crumb mixture on top. Bake 45 for minutes at 350°F.

SERVES 8–10.

Recipe courtesy of Randy Wayne White.

Cheesy Potatoes

Another delightful recipe from the collection of Lynda Leonard-Boyce. —RWW

    vegetable cooking spray

    4 medium potatoes, pared and sliced

    1 medium onion, sliced

    2 tablespoons butter, cut in small pieces

    salt and pepper

    3 tablespoons cream

    1 cup shredded cheddar cheese

Preheat grill to medium heat. Coat an aluminum foil pan with vegetable cooking spray. Place potato and onion slices in pan. Sprinkle with butter pieces and salt and pepper. Pour cream over vegetables. Top with shredded cheese. Cover pan tightly with aluminum foil. Place on grill for 30 to 35 minutes.

SERVES 4.

Recipe courtesy of Lynda Leonard-Boyce.

Fishing at sunset, Sanibel bay beach

Osprey with its catch

Georgia Style Candied Potatoes

If you like the taste of oranges you will love my Aunt Della Wilson Denison's version of this holiday dish. —RWW

6 medium sweet potatoes (cook until tender)

½ cup sugar

½ cup brown sugar, packed

½ cup orange juice

2 teaspoons vanilla

1 tablespoon corn syrup

1 tablespoon cornstarch

¼ teaspoon cinnamon

4 tablespoons butter

⅛ teaspoon salt

Peel and slice sweet potatoes. Add to 2½ quart greased casserole dish. Mix together sugar, brown sugar, orange juice, vanilla, corn syrup, cornstarch, cinnamon, butter and salt. Cook mixture for five minutes in a small pan until sauce thickens. Pour over potatoes. Bake uncovered for 30 minutes at 350°F.

SERVES 8.

Recipe courtesy of Randy Wayne White.

Georgia Wilson White's Creamed Onions

My mother and Carlene's mother always served creamed onions with Sunday and holiday dinners. Many Southern cooks also add ingredients such as dry sherry, nutmeg, grated Parmesan cheese, paprika, or dry mustard for creative varieties. —RWW

¼ cup butter

¼ cup flour

2 cups of light cream

salt and pepper

1 (15-ounce) jar whole onions, drained

vegetable cooking spray

Preheat oven to 350°F. Place butter in a medium saucepan over medium heat. When butter has melted, stir in flour to form a roux. Slowly add cream, stirring constantly until sauce thickens. Season with salt and pepper to taste. Add onions and stir until they are well coated with the sauce.

Pour onions and sauce into a medium baking dish that has been coated with vegetable cooking spray. Bake, uncovered, for 10 minutes or until mixture is bubbly.

SERVES 6.

Recipe courtesy of Randy Wayne White.

In the dark mass of shore, birds were beginning to make their morning sounds. A rooster crowed. Trees began to move in a freshening dawn wind.

—*Grand Cayman Siam*, RWW (as Randy Striker)

Cheesy Hash Brown Potatoes

I think most people have a cheesy potatoes recipe. If not I highly recommend my Aunt JoAnn Wilson Byers' version. Cooking with Velveeta cheese brings back childhood memories. —RWW

1 can cream of chicken soup

1 teaspoon salt

1 teaspoon pepper

1 (16–ounce) sour cream

1 pound Velveeta, cubed

1 (32–ounce) package frozen, diced, hash brown potatoes

1½ tubes Ritz crackers, crushed

1 stick butter, melted

Grease 13 x 9-inch casserole dish. Mix soup, salt, pepper and sour cream together. Add soup mixture and half the cheese to potatoes. Spread out in greased casserole dish. Cover top of potatoes with remaining cheese. Crush up 1½ tubes of Ritz crackers. Melt butter and mix with cracker crumbs. Sprinkle cracker crumb mixture on top. Bake at 350°F for 1 hour.

SERVES 8.

Recipe courtesy of Randy Wayne White.

Bonita Bill's docks, Matanzas Pass, and San Carlos Island's shrimp fleet in the distance

Beans and Rice

Perfect Beans

Red and black beans are daily fare in the homes of most families in Central America. Families with limited resources eat beans as a main dish three times a day, and wealthier families serve them as a side dish with full course meals.

Women cook beans by the potful and use them in a variety of dishes, adding various seasonings: cumin, chopped cilantro, chopped onions, green pepper, black or red pepper. Freshly cooked beans are served whole or pureed, sometimes topped with sour cream or finely shredded cheese, and accompanied by rice, salad, eggs, tortillas, or cooked bananas. Savory bean soups are prepared with some of the beans and excess cooking broth. Cooked beans can be refrigerated for five to seven days and quickly reheated for an easy meal or snack mixed with rice or pureed for refried beans. —RWW

> 1 pound dried red or black beans, sorted through, with broken ones discarded
>
> 3 slices bacon, diced
>
> 1 teaspoon salt
>
> 3 cloves garlic
>
> 1 tablespoon canola oil
>
> 1 to 2 beef bouillon cubes

Place beans in a large soup pot and add 2 quarts water to cover. Cover pot and allow beans to soak overnight.

Place a medium skillet over medium-high heat. Add bacon and fry, stirring frequently, until bacon is crispy. Remove with a slotted spoon and drain on paper toweling.

Place bean pot over high heat. Add salt, garlic, canola oil, bouillon, and bacon. When mixture comes to a boil, reduce heat to medium-low, cover pot, and simmer until beans are tender, about 2 hours.

SERVES 8.

Recipe courtesy of Randy Wayne White.

Perfect Rice

This rice has a marvelous aroma, and I've always had perfect results. —RWW

1 cup Cache River Basmati Popcorn rice or Cache River Brown Basmati Rice

1 teaspoon salt

1 tablespoon canola oil

2 cups of water

Place rice, salt, oil, and 2 cups water in a large saucepan over medium-high heat. Bring to a rolling boil. Cover, reduce heat to low, and simmer for 20 minutes.

Do not stir! Remove saucepan from heat and allow it to sit, covered, for 10 minutes.

MAKES 3 CUPS.

Recipe courtesy of Randy Wayne White.

Jasmine flowers sense the temperature change, and bloom. Nightfall pivots on the final orange axis of sunset, and, all up and down the islands, electric lights go on. To people on boats in Pine Island Sound, the pockets of light mark the night strongholds of human occupation in the mangrove darkness. —*The Heat Islands,* RWW

Chicken with Rice

Traveling to foreign countries has many advantages. I discovered this wonderful dish on one of my many trips to Colombia. —RWW

1 (3-pound) chicken, skinned and cut into serving pieces

2 tablespoons lemon juice

salt and pepper

¼ cup olive oil

1 onion, chopped

1 cup green bell pepper, chopped

3 cloves garlic, mashed

½ cup celery, chopped

¼ cup tomato paste

½ teaspoon ground cumin

¼ teaspoon dried oregano

2 cups uncooked rice

¼ teaspoon ground turmeric or saffron

2½ cups chicken broth

1 cup cooked peas

1 cup cooked, diced carrots (optional)

¼ cup roasted red peppers, finely chopped

Season chicken with lemon juice and salt and pepper to taste. Place olive oil in a large, deep skillet over medium-high heat. When oil is hot, add chicken and sauté, turning once, until browned. Remove chicken to a plate and set aside. Drain excess oil from skillet.

Return skillet to burner and add onion, green bell pepper, garlic, and celery. Sauté, stirring occasionally, until onion is transparent. Add tomato paste, cumin, oregano, and ¼ teaspoon black pepper. Stir to combine ingredients. Add rice and stir to combine.

Place browned chicken back in skillet. Add turmeric and 1 teaspoon salt to chicken broth and stir to mix. Pour broth over chicken in skillet. Cover skillet and bring liquid to a boil. Reduce heat to medium-low and simmer until rice is fluffy and chicken is cooked through, about 20 to 25 minutes.

Remove chicken to a plate. Add peas and carrots to rice mixture and stir to mix well. Transfer rice to a large serving platter. Place chicken atop rice. Sprinkle roasted red peppers atop chicken and rice.

SERVES 4 TO 6.

Recipe courtesy of Randy Wayne White.

. . . The moon was enormous over the Gulf of Mexico. It was a gaseous sphere, meteor scars showing, sitting on a rim of atmosphere that buffered Captiva Island from the emptiness of outer space. Beyond the bridge, white surf rolled out of a far horizon that touched the Yucatan and the jungles of Central America. —*Tampa Burn*, RWW

Sunset over Tarpon Bay

Consommé Rice

Lovely Aunt Johnsie Wilson Russo's simple but tasty rice dish goes well with a variety of meats and is a quick fix especially for families like mine who were always on the go. —RWW

1 cup extra long grain white rice

2 (10¾ ounce) cans of beef consommé soup, no water added

1 teaspoon butter

(½ cup onion, chopped, optional)

Mix together rice, consommé and butter. Heat on the stove over medium. Bring to a boil. Put into a greased 2 quart casserole dish, cover and bake for 30 minutes at 350°F, or until all liquid is absorbed. Let stand 5 minutes before serving.

SERVES 8.

Recipe courtesy of Randy Wayne White.

It was one of those common tropical nights that always seem too rare: moon-glazed sea, wind in the palms, the lights of boats blending with the glimmer of stars on the dark horizon.

—*Grand Cayman Siam*, RWW (as Randy Striker)

Nicaraguan Valencia Rice

I first visited Nicaragua in the late '70s and fell in love with the people and the food. The Mad Monk Stadium in Managua, Nicaragua, is a great place to watch baseball. —RWW

1 (2- to 3-pound) chicken

⅛ teaspoon pepper

1 teaspoon salt

1 carrot, peeled and diced

2 potatoes, peeled and diced

½ cup frozen peas

2½ tablespoons olive oil

1 medium onion chopped

½ cup chopped green bell pepper

1 stalk celery, chopped

2 cloves garlic, minced

2 cups uncooked short-grained Valencia rice

3 sprigs fresh mint or cilantro

½ cup tomato sauce

2 tablespoons white wine or white wine vinegar

1 tablespoon Worcestershire sauce

1 teaspoon prepared mustard

1 cup chopped cooked shrimp or 1 cup cubed ham

½ cup raisins

½ cup pitted and chopped green olives

Place chicken in a 4-quart saucepan and add water to cover. Place saucepan over medium-high heat. Add ⅛ teaspoon pepper and 1 teaspoon salt. Bring water to a boil, then reduce heat to medium-low, cover, and simmer until chicken is tender and cooked through. Remove chicken to a plate and allow it to cool.

Skim foam and fat from chicken broth. Increase heat to medium. Add carrot, potatoes, and peas to chicken broth. Cook until just tender, about 8 to 10 minutes. Remove saucepan from heat. Using a slotted spoon, remove vegetables to a plate. Allow chicken broth to cool.

Place olive oil in another 4-quart saucepan over medium heat. When oil is hot, add onion, bell pepper, celery, garlic, and rice. Sauté, stirring frequently, until rice is pearly white. Add 3 cups reserved chicken broth, 1 teaspoon salt, dash of pepper, and sprigs of herbs. Bring liquid to a boil, then reduce heat to low, cover, and simmer for 20 minutes.

Meanwhile, remove chicken meat from the bones, discarding skin and bones and tearing chicken into bite-size pieces. Place chicken and reserved vegetables in a large saucepan. Add tomato sauce, wine or vinegar, Worcestershire sauce, mustard, shrimp or ham, raisins, and olives. Toss to mix all ingredients well. Place saucepan over medium-low heat and cook, stirring frequently, until mixture is heated through.

Fluff rice with a fork. Add chicken mixture to rice and stir to mix. Remove saucepan from heat and cover. Allow the chicken and rice to rest for 10 to 20 minutes to marry flavors. Serve with warm tortillas, salad, or refried beans.

SERVES 4 TO 6.

Recipe courtesy of Randy Wayne White.

A Campeche wind was blowing off the Gulf, stirring the tops of palms. It leached a cumulative heat from the islands' sand face, weighted with the oder of seagrapes, palmetto, oak leaves, [and] prickly pear. —*Tampa Burn,* RWW

Bill "Spaceman" Lee, RWW, and son Rogan on the hunt for recipes in Cuba

CHAPTER 14

OUTDOOR COOKING

I watched the moon flatten itself over a black plateau of mangroves. Then the moon vaporized in a striated cloud of rust. —*Twelve Mile Limit*, RWW

Weekly Pig Roast

Each Saturday at sunset, the fishing guides and the live-aboards throw money in a pot to finance Dinkin's Bay weekly Pig Roast and Beer Cotillion. The name is misleading because pigs and cotillions don't play a role. Beer, however, does. Ice is shoveled into Igloos, and the beer is buried deep. Kelly, from the takeout, loads the picnic table over by the seagrape tree with platters of shrimp and fried conch and anything else that happens to be lying around the kitchen. The live-aboards begin socializing on the docks, freshly showered and drinks in hand at sunset. Which is usually about the time the guides finish washing down their skiffs.

For the first hour or so, it's marina community only. No wandering tourists allowed, no locals looking for a free meal. There is a chain-link gate on the shell road that leads to the marina, and Mack keeps the gate closed. But after all the food has been eaten, and if there's still enough beer, Mack strolls out and opens the gate. After that, the length of the party is commensurated with the endurance of marina residents and outsiders alike.

—*Captiva*, RWW

Celebration time
at Tarpon Bay
Marina

Kabobs

Select quick-cooking foods like cubes of chicken or tender steak, tomatoes, green peppers, mushrooms, small potatoes, onions. (To use less-tender cuts of beef, use marinade or meat tenderizer.)

When different kinds of food share the same skewer, choose only those that will cook in the same length of time and that are approximately the same size. In cubing meat, or cutting up vegetables, make pieces even.

Leave a little space between foods on the skewer, so heat can reach all surfaces. If you like, for beef kabobs cooked rare, push foods close together.

Brush vegetables with melted butter or margarine, or salad oil, before and during skewer cooking. If you used a marinade on the meat, baste with it now and then.

Cook kabobs over hot coals so food stays moist, yet browns evenly.

To remove food from the skewer, point it down at plate, use a 2-tined fork above the 2 or 3 chunks of food nearest the tip, and push off. Repeat. This way, vegetables don't get squashed.

Recipe courtesy of Randy Wayne White.

Hickory Barbecued Ribs

These ribs are great as they are, and better if you have a real smoker. The trick is to cook slowly, and do not add sauce until the ribs are done. —RWW

4 pounds meaty loin back ribs or 3 racks spareribs

1 cup chopped onion

¼ cup canola oil

1 (8-ounce) can seasoned tomato sauce

½ cup water

¼ cup brown sugar

¼ cup lemon juice

3 tablespoons Worcestershire sauce

2 tablespoons prepared mustard

2 teaspoons salt

¼ teaspoon pepper

Lace ribs on spit accordion-style, using holding forks. Adjust on rotisserie above drip pan. Let ribs rotate over slow coals.

Cook onion in hot oil until tender. Add remaining ingredients; simmer uncovered 15 minutes. After ribs cook 40 minutes, baste well with the sauce; add damp hickory to coals. Cook 20 minutes longer or until well-done (no pink when snipped between bones).

If you use spareribs:

Have the meat man saw them into 2 strips. Beginning with narrow end of ribs, lace on spit accordion-style. Start second strip at wide end, third at narrow end. Have a holding fork for each slab of ribs.

SERVES 4 TO 6.

Recipe courtesy of Randy Wayne White.

The water is light—saturated, a radiant gel that diffuses the neat boundaries of sea and space, creating pale demarcations of color. Everything is luminous, nothing is defined. —*The Sharks of Lake Nicaragua*, RWW

Fish shack in Pine Island Sound

Casa del Fuego BBQ Shrimp

Paula Berry says this is an excellent appetizer, or even a main course if you make enough. The secret is in the sauce and slow grilling. They do like attention at the grill, but your efforts will be worth it. —RWW

1 pound lean bacon (20 slices)

2 pounds large Florida pink shrimp (about 40), peeled and deveined

1 (16-ounce) jar Bone Suckin' Sauce, mild or hot paprika (can be purchased locally at the Pine Island U-Pick on Pine Island Road)

pepper

10 long metal skewers

Pre-brown bacon. Bring bacon to room temperature. Cut bacon in half. Wrap a half-slice bacon around each shrimp, covering the entire surface. Skewer 4 bacon-wrapped shrimp onto each metal skewer, leaving ½-inch space between shrimp.

Season skewered shrimp with paprika sauce and pepper to taste. Place on a platter, cover with aluminum foil, and refrigerate until ready to grill.

Heat gas grill to medium-low temperature. Place skewered shrimp on grill. (Keep a close watch on shrimp, because dripping bacon grease may cause a flare-up.) Cook shrimp until crisp, turning shrimp frequently until bacon is cooked thoroughly and browned.

Keeping grill at as low a temperature as possible, when bacon is browned, begin basting with barbecue sauce, turning skewers frequently. Continue cooking until sauce is caramelized and bacon is sweet and crunchy.

SERVES 10 AS AN APPETIZER.

Recipe courtesy of Paula Berry, Useppa Island Fire Rescue.

There are subtleties of color, scent, and sound that can only be appreciated out-doors, which is why almost everyone heads for the beach or the bay. —*Dead of Night*, RWW

Charcoal Grilled Grouper with Mango Butter

The combination of charcoal grilled grouper together with mango butter is a tropical delight. —RWW

1 pound butter, at room temperature

1 small ripe mango, peeled, seeded, and pureed

1 ripe banana, peeled and pureed

zest of 1 orange

10 ounces white wine

juice of 1 orange

1 bunch fresh mint, finely chopped

cinnamon

3 egg yolks

6 (8-ounce) grouper fillets

¼ cup melted butter

seasoned salt

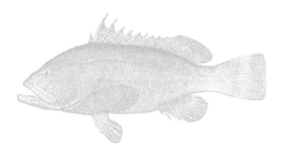

Place butter in bowl of an electric mixer. Beat until light and fluffy. Place mango, banana, and orange zest in a small bowl. Stir to mix.

Place white wine, orange juice, and mint in a medium saucepan over high heat. Bring mixture to a boil and reduce to ⅓ cup. Remove from heat and allow it to cool. Add liquid to fruit mixture and stir to combine. Add cinnamon to taste. Add egg yolks and whisk to mix well. Add fruit mixture to whipped butter in bowl of electric mixer. Mix together on low speed until smooth. Set aside.

Build a charcoal fire or preheat gas grill. Using a pastry brush, brush fillets with melted butter. Sprinkle both sides of grouper fillets with seasoned salt. Grill fillets for 10 minutes per inch of thickness or until fish flakes when tested with a fork.

To serve, place 1 grouper fillet on each of 6 dinner plates. Top each with a dollop of mango butter.

SERVES 6.

Recipe courtesy of The Mucky Duck on Captiva.

LIVE MUSIC
By
TONY COPELAND

APPLE BOBBING CONTEST

* DOOR PRIZES *

BOAT RIDES
ON
THE ISLAND BELLE

SPECIAL SALES

TARPON BAY MARINA
(Bay End of Tarpon Bay Road)
ON SANIBEL ISLAND

RED PELICAN
FASHION SHOW

**RED WHITE AND BLUE
COUNTRY WEEKEND**
July 2nd and 3rd

CLOWNS

* PIG ROAST *
Complete Dinners only $5.95
Free Drinks with Lunch and Dinner

PRIZES FOR:

Canoe Races
Horse Shoe Pitching Contest
Buffalo Chip Throwing Contest
Watermelon Seed Spitting Contest

BALLOONS

BANJO PICKIN' and FIDDLING
CONTESTS

FUN FOR THE WHOLE FAMILY!

Fliers were passed out for Tarpon Bay Marina events.

The rain hadn't reached me yet, but the wind was fierce. A Halloween moon rose above a tower of cumulus clouds. My island had taken on a strange new look. It was no longer a place of tin-roofed houses built upon Indian shell mounds. Tonight, it was a black mass elevated over the water, a dinosaur-shape afloat. —*A Gold Medallion*, RWW

The autumn days were hot and calm; perfect days for slow love and cold beer and talk. —*The Deep Six*, RWW

(Left) Enjoying a beer during Happy Hour on Sanibel. (Below) I meet the nicest people in Sanibel and Captiva restaurants.

Foods Cooked in Beer

Beer; frankly, I admire it. —RWW

Thirsty for Beer

In April, Sanibel and Captiva Islands are as crowded and animated as any Carnival cruise ship, but with a basic difference. People who come to the islands tend to be like-minded, outdoors oriented, and energized by a longing for quiet beaches and immersion in the subtropics: wading birds, gators, crocs, manatees, littoral fish, coconut palms, ospreys—you name it. Look at the people who come year after year, who make the islands part of their lives, and you will think of L.L. Bean catalogs. You'll think of *Audubon* magazine. Or maybe *Outside.* The fact that the islands maintain more wild space than hotel space is precisely why they continue to be so widely treasured.

Which is the reason I don't mind getting out into the tourist rush occasionally, eating dinner at a favorite restaurant. The people you meet are usually pretty nice. Interesting, too.

Tomlinson came tapping at my door at twilight, looking dapper in blue jeans and silk Hawaiian shirt, pink flamingos and golden tiki huts thereon, his bony hands offering two cold bottles of beer.

"It's very important to rehydrate in this hellish spring heat," he explained. "But if you want to wait for dinner, I'll drink both bottles. Waste is a terrible thing. As we speak, there are Christian alcoholics absolutely jonesing for a drink in places like Iraq and Libya. Parts of . . . somewhere else, too. Arkansas? Yeah, probably Arkansas. I'm telling you just in case you feel like refusing this beverage."

I took one of the beers from him. "Nope, I'm thirsty."

"Just checking."

—*The Mangrove Coast,* RWW

Brisket in Beer

Beer is a wonderful ingredient and I use it a lot in my cooking. —RWW

1 (3-pound) beef brisket (thick cut)

1 (12-ounce) bottle Heinz Premium chili sauce

1 (12-ounce) can beer

8 ounces water

salt and pepper

3 carrots, peeled and cut into 1½-inch chunks

3 stalks celery, cut into 2-inch pieces

2 onions, thinly sliced

6 potatoes, peeled and quartered

Preheat oven to 350°F. Place brisket in a roasting pan, fat side up. Mix chili sauce, beer and 8 ounces water together in a medium bowl. Pour mixture over brisket. Season with salt and pepper to taste. Cook brisket for 3 hours. Two hours before meat is done add carrots, celery, onions and potatoes.

SERVES 4 TO 6.

Another recipe from Claire Baum. Courtesy of Carlene Fredericka Brennen.

Captiva Cajun Beer Batter for Shrimp

This recipe is from Captain Lamar Williams, who charters out of Jensen's Twin Palm Resort and Marina on Captiva. This lovely small resort is owned and managed by three of my favorite people— the Jensen brothers, Dave, John, and Jimmy. Jensen's Marina appears often in my books. They have their own marina band, the Trouble Starters, and some of the most interesting people from the islands congregate there. —RWW

1 cup all-purpose flour

1 teaspoon baking soda

1 teaspoon cream of tartar

¼ cup blackening seasoning

2 (12-ounce) beers

2 pounds medium-size Florida pink
   shrimp, peeled and deveined

Remoulade Sauce:

1 cup mayonnaise

¼ cup capers

juice of ½ lemon

pepper

Mix all dry ingredients together. Whisk in beer until lumps are gone. Coat peeled shrimp well. Drop in hot grease (350°F). Shake fryer basket so batter does not stick. Cook until golden brown. Serve with remoulade sauce.

For the remoulade sauce: Blend all ingredients, but do not puree.

SERVES 4.

Recipe courtesy of Captain Lamar Williams.

Alaskan Snow Crab Clusters Cooked in Beer

Carlene's friend Lynda Leonard-Boyce boils her crab legs in beer. A woman after my own heart. —RWW

4 Alaskan snow crab clusters, thawed

36 ounces beer

Place crab and beer in a large pot over medium heat. Add enough water to cover crab clusters. Bring to a boil and cook 5 to 10 minutes. Drain and serve with melted butter.

SERVES 4.

Recipe courtesy of Lynda Leonard-Boyce.

San Carlos Bay, with Sanibel Island and the
lighthouse in the distance

CHAPTER 15

ISLAND DESSERTS

. . . The first smear of daylight hung foglike over Sulphur Wells . . . then expanded out of the Pine Island tree line: a stratum of gray membrane that, gradually, was streaked with conch pink and violet. Somewhere over Bimini, maybe: someplace in the Bahamas chain—the sun was wheeling around the rim of earth, moving incrementally across the Gulf Stream toward Florida. —*Everglades*, RWW

Coconut Island Pie

Every Southerner has to have a coconut pie recipe. My mother made wonderful pies, including a coconut pie that was a family favorite. Lynda Leonard-Boyce has a terrific pie recipe. You can make it yourself or stop by the Sanibel Café for a slice. —RWW

3 eggs

3 tablespoons flour

1½ cups sugar

1 cup shredded sweetened coconut

1 cup crushed pineapple, drained

½ cup melted butter

1 (9-inch) piecrust, unbaked

1 cup whipped cream

2 tablespoons shredded sweetened coconut

Coconut palms on Captiva Island

Preheat oven to 365°F. Place eggs in the bowl of an electric mixer. Beat until frothy. Reduce mixer speed to low and slowly fold in flour, sugar, coconut, and pineapple. Add melted butter and mix until batter is smooth. Pour batter into unbaked piecrust. Bake 40 to 45 minutes or until filling is set and crust is lightly browned.

To serve, top with whipped cream and a sprinkling of shredded coconut.

SERVES 6 TO 8.

Recipe courtesy of Lynda Leonard-Boyce.

Dan's Sanibel Rum Cake

Dan Toolan is a good friend of Carlene's. His rum cake is always a hit at island parties and during the holidays. —RWW

Cake:

1 package Betty Crocker Super Moist yellow cake mix

¼ cup plus ½ tablespoon water

½ cup plus 4 teaspoons canola oil

3 eggs

¼ cup dark rum

vegetable cooking spray

Glaze:

1 stick butter

5 tablespoons light or dark brown sugar

½ cup rum

1 tablespoon powdered sugar (optional)

For the cake:

Preheat oven to 350°F. Place cake mix, water, oil, eggs, and ¼ cup rum in the large bowl of an electric mixer. Beat on low speed for 30 seconds, then on medium speed for 2 minutes, scraping bowl occasionally. Coat a Bundt pan with vegetable cooking spray. Pour batter into pan. Bake for 38 to 43 minutes, or until a wooden skewer inserted in the center comes out clean. Cool cake in pan for 15 minutes.

For the glaze:

Meanwhile, place butter, brown sugar, and ½ cup rum into a small saucepan over medium-low heat. Cook, stirring constantly, until butter is melted, sugar has dissolved, and mixture is well blended.

Pour glaze over cake in Bundt pan. Allow cake to rest for about 7 minutes so glaze can soak in. Place serving plate upside down on top of Bundt pan and quickly invert cake onto plate. Remove pan. Dust cake with powdered sugar.

SERVES 8 TO 10.

Recipe courtesy of Dan Toolan.

Fresh Mango Yogurt with Blueberries and Banana

This is a favorite dessert from the Nutmeg House on Sanibel. Although the restaurant has closed its doors, Carlene still serves this dish at home. —RWW

2 large mangoes, peeled and pitted

1½ teaspoons honey

1 teaspoon vanilla extract

3 cups plain vanilla yogurt

1 pint blueberries

3 bananas, peeled and sliced

6 large strawberries

Place 1 mango in a blender or food processor and puree until smooth. Transfer to a large bowl. Coarsely chop the other mango and set aside.

Add honey to mango puree and stir until honey dissolves. Mix in ½ cup of the chopped mango. Gently fold in vanilla extract, yogurt, 1 cup blueberries, and half the sliced bananas. Divide yogurt mixture among 6 individual chilled bowls. Sprinkle each bowl with the remaining chopped mango and blueberries. Top with remaining bananas and place a strawberry in the middle of each serving.

SERVES 6.

Key Lime Pie

The Mucky Duck is one of Captiva's most beloved restaurants. Not only do they have great food, but it is a fun place to dine thanks to owner Victor Mayeron and his friendly staff. Their wonderful Key Lime Pie or sunset (or both) at The Mucky Duck are worth the drive. —RWW

    3 egg yolks

    3½ ounces Key lime juice

    8 ounces sweetened condensed milk, like Eagle brand

    3 egg whites

    1 (9-inch) graham-cracker piecrust

    1 cup heavy cream, whipped

    Key lime slices for garnish

Place egg yolks in a large bowl. Whisk in Key lime juice and condensed milk. Place egg whites in the bowl of an electric mixer and beat until stiff. Using a spoon, gently fold egg whites into the Key lime mixture, taking care not to deflate the beaten whites. Pour Key lime mixture into piecrust and freeze until solid.

To serve: Top each serving with a dollop of whipped cream and garnish with a slice of Key lime. Serve frozen.

SERVES 6 TO 8.

Recipe courtesy of The Mucky Duck on Captiva.

. . . bright moon and frozen stars against a black tropical sky. A meteor flared through the darkness and faded. —*Grand Cayman Siam*, RWW (as Randy Striker)

Roseate spoonbills in the J. N. "Ding" Darling National Wildlife Refuge

Old-Fashioned White Sheet Cake with White or Chocolate Icing

Sheet cakes were popular desserts when I was a youngster. Each happy event was a chance to celebrate, to bring the family together and you could always count on sweet Aunt Jewel Wilson McRae to bring one of her delicious sheet cakes to the gathering. —RWW

2½ cups sifted flour

1 teaspoon baking powder

1 teaspoon salt

1½ cups sugar

½ cup shortening

1 cup milk

3 eggs

1 teaspoon vanilla

White Icing

2 cups powdered sugar

¼ cup milk

½ teaspoon vanilla

Sift together flour, baking powder, salt, and sugar. Add shortening and milk. Add eggs, 1 teaspoon vanilla and beat for 2 minutes. Pour into a lightly greased, floured 16 x 11-inch pan or 3 layer pans. Bake for 25–30 minutes at 350°F.

Icing

In bowl mix sugar, milk and vanilla. If you want chocolate icing add ¼ cup cocoa.

SERVES 10.

Recipe courtesy of Randy Wayne White.

Bananas in Paradise

Shirley's Spirit of Foolishness on Captiva was known for this wonderful dessert. Carlene called Shirley's establishment a true island dining experience. The restaurant's closing saddened the hearts of many islanders. —RWW

1 (14-ounce) burrito-size flour tortillas

2 whole bananas

½ cup chopped mixed nuts

½ cup cold green grapes, cut into quarters

vegetable cooking spray

2 large scoops rum-raisin ice cream (or your favorite flavor)

1 cup whipped cream

Preheat oven to 500°F. Lay each tortilla flat and place a whole banana on the lower third. Sprinkle each banana with ¼ cup nuts. Top each with ¼ cup cold grapes. Roll tortilla, folding in the edges, until banana is completely covered. Spray thoroughly with vegetable cooking spray.

Place rolled bananas on a baking sheet and bake for 5 to 7 minutes, turning several times, until tortilla has lightly browned and is slightly crispy. Place each rolled banana in an individual shallow bowl. Top each with a scoop of ice cream and a generous dollop of whipped cream.

SERVES 2.

I was blessed by two Santeña priests.

Chocolate Pecan Pie

One of The Lighthouse Café's most popular desserts, especially for chocolate lovers. —RWW

1 (9-inch) unbaked piecrust

6 ounces mini chocolate chips

1½ cups pecan pieces

¼ cup melted butter

½ cup light corn syrup

½ cup sugar

2 large eggs, lightly beaten

Preheat oven to 325°F. Bake piecrust for 10 minutes. Remove crust from oven and allow it to cool. Line bottom of piecrust with chocolate chips. Place pecan pieces atop chocolate chips.

Place butter, corn syrup, sugar, and eggs in a small bowl. Whisk ingredients until smooth. Pour mixture over pecans in crust. Bake for 45 minutes. (If edges of piecrust get too brown, cover with narrow strips of aluminum foil.)

SERVES 6 TO 8.

Recipe courtesy of The Lighthouse Café on Sanibel Island.

It was summer dusk and mosquitoes were moving over the water out of mangrove shadows. Light in the Western sky beyond the mangroves beyond the marina, had an oyster sheen. High clouds to the east still reflected a rusty, mango band of sunset upon cumulous canyons. —*Tampa Burn*, RWW

Texas Sheet Cake

Carlene told me this is one of her favorite dessert recipes in the cookbook. She has served it to family and friends with great success. My beloved mother Georgia Wilson White was used to receiving compliments for her baking and this cake recipe was one of her favorites. Mine too. —RWW

2 cups self-rising flour

1½ cups sugar

½ teaspoon salt

1 teaspoon baking soda

2 sticks butter (or margarine)

1 cup water

4 tablespoons cocoa

2 eggs, beaten

½ cup buttermilk (or milk)

1 teaspoon vanilla

Frosting:

1 stick of butter (or margarine)

4 tablespoons cocoa

6 tablespoons of milk

1 box of powdered sugar, sifted

½ teaspoon vanilla

Sift together and set aside: flour, sugar, salt, and baking soda. Bring to a boil: 2 sticks of butter, water, and 4 tablespoons of cocoa. In a small bowl beat: eggs, buttermilk, and 1 teaspoon of vanilla. Add water mixture to flour mixture. Add egg mixture. Mix well. Pour into either a greased and floured 17x1x1 jelly roll pan (for thinner cake) and bake for 15–20 minutes at 350°F or 13 x 9-inch baking pan and bake for 22 minutes at 375°F.

Frosting

Bring to boil butter, cocoa, and milk. Pour over one box of sifted powdered sugar. Mix and add ½ teaspoon of vanilla. Frost while still warm. Frosting will be thin.

SERVES UP TO 24.

Recipe courtesy of Randy Wayne White.

Easy & Delicious Cookies

My mother Georgia Wilson White was a well respected baker. Her cookie recipes never went out of style. Everyone who ever ate one of these cookie bars not only wanted more but usually went home with the recipe. —RWW

1 stick butter, melted

1½ cups graham cracker crumbs

1 (6-ounce) package chocolate chips

1 (6-ounce) package of butterscotch chips

1 cup (finely shredded) sweetened coconut

1 cup pecans, chopped

1 (14-ounce) can sweetened condensed milk, like Eagle brand

Melt butter and mix with graham cracker crumbs. Spread on the bottom of a greased 9 x 13-inch pan. Add in layers chocolate chips, butterscotch chips, coconut, pecans—do not stir! Pour condensed milk over mixture. Bake for 25–35 minutes at 325°F. Cool and cut into bars.

MAKES 20 BARS.

Recipe courtesy of Randy Wayne White.

Nuttie Fingers

My Aunt Jewel Wilson McRae loved to bake. Actually we are all bakers. This recipe was a popular request for family celebrations. Because these cookies are so light I tend to eat more than I should. —RWW

2 cups of cake flour

7 tablespoons powdered sugar

⅛ teaspoon salt

1½ sticks of butter (or margarine)

2 teaspoons vanilla

1 tablespoon ice water

1½ cups pecans, finely chopped

More powdered sugar for rolling

Sift together flour, sugar, and salt. Cut butter into flour mixture using a food processor, 2 knives or a pastry blender. Add vanilla, ice water, and pecans and mix well. Roll cookies into skinny logs–size of your finger. Don't make them too long. Place on a parchment paper-lined cookie sheet. Bake for 15 minutes at 350°F. Let cool just slightly and remove to wire racks. Roll in powdered sugar. Return to wire rack to cool completely.

MAKES ABOUT 3 DOZEN COOKIES.

Recipe courtesy of Randy Wayne White.

Oreo Balls

To speed up the process of making one of my favorite desserts, I would do the first two steps of this recipe using a food processor. I'm sure my Aunt Della Wilson Denson would approve. Saving time in the kitchen was always important to the women in my family. —RWW

> 1 package Oreo cookies
>
> 1 (8-ounce) package cream cheese
>
> 1 pound package Candy Quick / Almond Bark Chocolate Coating

Crush Oreo cookies (to the consistency of graham cracker crumbs). Mix in entire package of cream cheese until it forms a paste. Roll into balls about the size of a quarter. Melt chocolate over water on low heat or in the microwave. Coat Oreo Balls in the chocolate and set on wax paper. Put in refrigerator until set.

MAKES ABOUT 30.

Recipe courtesy of Randy Wayne White.

The sea changed from the strain of darkness with dawn and in graduation of fresh light. In the east, the blackness lifted in an airy white corona and the breeze freshened. —*Cuban Death-Lift*, RWW (as Randy Striker)

Sweet Potato Pie

No holiday dinner in our house was complete without my grandmother Nayrilla Wilson's Sweet Potato Pie. —RWW

3 large sweet potatoes

3 tablespoon self-rising flour

¾ teaspoon nutmeg

1 teaspoon cinnamon

1 teaspoon vanilla

3 eggs, separated (save whites for meringue topping)

½ cup sugar

¾ cup evaporated milk, like Carnation brand

½ stick butter, melted

Meringue:

3 egg whites

5 tablespoons of sugar

Bake sweet potatoes for 1 hour to 1 hour and 15 minutes at 350°F or until done. Peel potatoes, dice, and put in mixer bowl. Add butter to bowl. Add 3 tablespoons of self-rising flour, nutmeg, cinnamon, and vanilla. Separate 3 eggs (save whites if you want meringue). Mix egg yolks, sugar and evaporated milk and add to potato mixture. Whip until smooth. Pour into greased pie pan. Bake for 40 minutes at 350°F, or until light brown. Whisk egg whites and sugar in mixer till stiff. Cover the pie to the edge with meringue and bake for 15–18 minutes, at 350°F until lightly browned.

SERVES 6–8.

Recipe courtesy of Randy Wayne White.

Date Nut Balls

My Aunt Jewel Wilson McRae's delicious date nut balls are chewy treats for any holiday. They are also easy to make. —RWW

1 stick butter (or margarine)

1 cup brown sugar

1 (8–ounce) package dates, chopped

3 cups crisped rice cereal, like Rice Krispies

1 cup pecans, chopped

½ cup (finely shredded) sweetened coconut

Combine and cook the butter, brown sugar and dates on low heat until dates dissolve. Add rice cereal, pecans and coconut. Mix well. Cool. Roll into small balls, roll each ball in powdered sugar. Place on wax paper.

MAKES ABOUT 50.

Recipe courtesy of Randy Wayne White.

The southernmost west coast of Florida is unlike anything else the vacation state has left to offer. It is vast mangrove forests, trees eighty feet high, and dark tidal rivers and uncharted oyster bars where the tides have ebbed and flowed for a thousand years. —*Key West Connection,* RWW

A great egret looking
for his next meal

STRESS RELIEF
$2.00
ASK BARTENDER
OR SERVER

CHAPTER 16

TROPICAL DRINKS

It was Friday night, cleanup and cocktail time. Fishing guides hosed their skiffs after working the late tide and live-aboards were beginning to circulate among neighboring houseboats, drinks in hand, smiles fixed, everybody smelling of shampoos and looking for a party. Someone had put speakers out on the dock so that Jimmy Buffett seemed to be erupting from the water, singing that, on the day that John Wayne died, he'd been on the Continental Divide. —*Sanibel Flats*, RWW

Drinks Worth Almost Dying For

Thanks to five new American friends, I may have discovered the perfect way to travel. Yesterday we rented a pickup truck in Belize City, then we each contributed $50 to a group fund. From the fund, we purchased coolers, ice, food, and bottled beverages. When the money was gone, we each contributed more money. Result: no bookkeeping, plus the back of the truck is loaded with comfortable seats (the coolers), plus many interesting things to drink. Among the *bebidas* (drinks) were a couple of fifths of a cheap *campesino* rum and a local, sediment-rich, ten-day beer which was prone to popping off its own lids when the temperature was above 80 degrees. And above 80 degrees was usually by 8:00 a.m. in Belize and Guatemala.

Riding in the back of a truck through the Maya Mountains (which extend from Belize into Guatemala) is a wonderful thing. The smells of river sloughs, of village cooking fires, of mountain cloud forests hit one full in the face, and children, standing beside their mothers washing clothes in fast rivers, grin at us and shout in Mayan. The only bad thing is that village militias spot us easily, and we are often detained at roadblocks by stern government troops who frisk us and paw through our bags.

Our trip was stalled at dusk when more than a dozen armed men—government militia—stepped out of the bushes, stopped our truck, and searched us. Coincidentally, our last spare tire went flat at the same time. Not so coincidentally, we ran out of bottled beverages about an hour later. These soldiers were not bad guys, and they apologized for the thoroughness of their earlier search. Clearly, though, we were in a tough spot here. We were out of beer. Also we needed to find a tire. But first things first.

One of the soldiers confided in us that he knew the local guerrilla leader who, he was certain, would sell us some beer. I am not an expert in politics, but visiting a guerrilla leader in the dead of night with a government soldier as a guide did not seem a good plan. But given the seriousness of the matter, we immediately set off on foot. There was no moon, but there were stars through the trees, and we followed the dirt road for more than a mile until we came to a thatched-roof hut that also served as a local tienda.

The soldier pounded on the door until the guerrilla leader answered, carrying a lighted candle. One of my demented new friends said to the soldier, "Tell this guy that if he doesn't sell us some beer, we'll kill this cow." He was pointing to a donkey tied beneath a tree, but it didn't matter because neither the soldier nor the storekeeper understood him.

The man sold us forty bottles of beer, which he separated into two burlap bags. Almost twenty bottles made it back to the truck. "It was all he had," I explained to the others. The trip ended well, and I think that it doesn't much matter how you hit the open road—just as long as you occasionally hit it. If you drive, do it sober!
—RWW

Randy Wayne White's Margarita

I like to serve a variety of drinks in canning jars with lids. It is not just delicious, but it's also really good exercise. —RWW

1½ ounces of tequila

1 ounce triple sec

juice from 2 fresh limes

sea salt

Lime slice or mint to garnish

Place tequila, triple sec, and lime juice in canning jar with ice. Add water to taste and a pinch of sea salt. Tighten lid and shake vigorously. Serve with lime or mint garnish.

SERVES 1.

Recipe courtesy of Randy Wayne White.

Alligators in the J. N. "Ding" Darling National Wildlife Refuge

Walden Pond Bloody Mary

I love this Bloody Mary. I got the recipe from Jim, the bartender at the Walden Grille in Concord, Massachusetts. I was in the Boston area, writing and narrating our documentary about taking baseball gear to kids in Cuba, *Gift of the Game.* Every day after work, I'd swim across Henry David Thoreau's Walden Pond, then stop at the Grille and chat with the locals. —RWW

1 (1½-ounce) shot Guinness

1 big (2-ounce) shot vodka

½ teaspoon prepared horseradish

good shake of black pepper

squeeze of fresh lime

kosher salt

2 tablespoons beef bouillon

3 teaspoons Worcestershire sauce

1 to 2 dashes Doc Ford's Green Flash Hot Sauce (available at www.docford .com)

V8 juice

1 spear cooked asparagus

jalapeño olives

1 cooked shrimp with tail

Fill a tall glass with ice. Add Guinness, vodka, horseradish, black pepper, lime, salt to taste, beef bouillon, Worcestershire sauce, and hot sauce. Stir well. Add V8 to top of glass. Stir again. Garnish with asparagus spear, jalapeño olives, and/or shrimp.

SERVES 1.

Recipe courtesy of Randy Wayne White.

Maggie Graham, Sue Gray, and Carlene Fredericka Brennen

Vodka-Oyster Shooters

Since we are dealing with raw oysters for this recipe, you need to be on good terms with a well-respected seafood market with which you are willing to trust your physical and mental well-being for that day, and probably the following week. Because if you don't, that's how long you and your unhappy guests will be living with your mistake. —RWW

Add tomato juice, horseradish, and pepper (to taste) in a blender. Pulse to mix thoroughly. Pour ½ shot (¾ ounce) of tomato-juice mixture into a small glass. Add a shot (1½ ounces) of vodka. Add 1 raw oyster to the glass and garnish with a squeeze of lemon.

SERVES 12.

Recipe courtesy of Randy Wayne White.

From the high regions of the Earth's atmosphere, a great volume of polar air, ascending because of its own density, caught the jet-stream push of what meteorologists call the five-hundred-millibar surface, and it began to drift southward toward the 26th parallel. By the evening,—the polar edge had gathered sufficient momentum to gravitate toward and then displace the warmer, lighter air of the tropics, and it arrived in south Florida as a blustering cold front driven by a wind that seemed to howl down out of the full moon. —*The Man Who Invented Florida*, RWW

Sunset over Sanibel Island

There are reasons why I don't like being away from home at sunset, some personal, most social. On the islands, sunset is ceremonial. It's the convivial, kicked back, communal time when even strangers become a little friendlier, and the world shifts collective gears, slowing its orbit in the growing, slow dusk. —*Dead of Night*, RWW

Doc Ford's Captiva Sunrise

I like this rummy's variation of a Bloody Mary. The recipe is from Granada, Nicaragua, a beautiful, old city on the shore of Lake Nicaragua. The city's a great place to base a rainforest exploration, or to just sit back and drink a few of these, available at Doc Ford's Sanibel Rum Bar & Grille. —RWW

2 ounces of your favorite rum

1 teaspoon prepared horseradish

3 dashes of Worcestershire sauce

dash of lime juice

3 dashes celery salt

3 dashes black pepper

tomato juice

1 lime slice

Fill a tall glass with ice. Add rum, horseradish, Worcestershire sauce, lime juice, celery salt, and black pepper. Add tomato juice to fill glass. Stir well. Garnish with slice of lime and enjoy a beautiful sunset.

SERVES 1.

Recipe courtesy of Randy Wayne White.

Doc Ford's Hemingway Daiquiri

This recipe is straight from our last baseball tour of Havana. The bartender at the La Floridita—Constante—invented it. La Floridita was Ernest Hemingway's favorite watering hole. Hemingway would come in after a day of fishing and order a "Papa," which was a double daiquiri. Doc Ford's Hemingway is a mélange of light rum, lime juice, grapefruit juice, and maraschino liqueur. Available at Doc Ford's Sanibel Rum Bar & Grille. —RWW

1½ ounces light rum

¾ ounce lime juice

¼ ounce grapefruit juice

¼ ounce maraschino liqueur

Place all ingredients in a blender. Fill blender with ice. Pulse until smooth and frothy.

SERVES 1.

Recipe courtesy of Doc Ford's Sanibel Rum Bar & Grille.

Sunset is always cocktail time on the island.

Doc Ford's Island Mojito

Sanibel is closer to Havana than to Miami. Only 197 nautical miles! Smell sugarcane and lime on the south wind! That's Cuba, home of the mojito (pronounced mo-HEE-to): a double shot of white rum, muddled fresh mint, local lime, raw sugar, and club soda. Perfect at Doc Ford's! —RWW

    2 ounces soda water

    1½ ounces simple syrup or sugar water

    4 sprigs fresh mint

    3 ounces rum

    fresh squeezed juice from ½ lime

Mix soda water, syrup, and fresh muddled (crushed) mint in a glass. Add ice, then rum. Cover with lid and shake.

SERVES 1.

> Recipe courtesy of Doc Ford's Sanibel Rum Bar & Grill, home of the Island Mojito.

Sanibel Beer Buster

Beer was the most popular beverage at the Tarpon Bay Marina Friday night parties. —RWW

    2 ounces 100-proof vodka

    3 dashes Doc Ford's Green Flash Hot Sauce (available at: www.rwwhite.com)

    1 (12-ounce) beer of choice

Place vodka and hot sauce in a tall beer stein or beer mug. Fill with your favorite beer. Do not stir.

SERVES 1.

> Recipe courtesy of Randy Wayne White.

Carlene's Golden Margarita

This is Carlene's favorite cocktail. According to Carlene, her good friend Dan Toolan of Sanibel Island makes the best golden margarita she has ever tasted. —RWW

1½ ounces Jose Cuervo Gold Tequila	Florida orange juice
½ ounce Grand Marnier	sea salt
½ ounce Key lime juice	lime wedge
3 ounces Jose Cuervo Margarita Mix	

Place tequila, Grand Marnier, Key lime juice, margarita mix, and a generous splash of orange juice in a large shaker and fill with ice. Cover and shake until frothy and well mixed. Rub rim of a margarita glass with salt. Pour drink into salted glass. Garnish with lime wedge.

SERVES 1.

Recipe courtesy of Carlene Fredericka Brennen.

Sanibel Sunrise

This was a popular drink at Wil's Landing on Sanibel, where the business community congregated. A memory from the past. —RWW

¾ ounce vodka	cranberry juice
¾ ounce light rum	7UP
¾ ounce triple sec	lime wedge

Fill a tall glass with ice. Add vodka, rum, and triple sec. Add cranberry juice to within 1 inch of rim. Cover with lid and shake. Add a splash of 7UP and a squeeze of lime.

(Add ¾ ounce gin to liquors in this drink to make the Wil's Landing signature drink, the Sanibel Slammer.)

SERVES 1.

Recipe courtesy of Wil Schlosser.

Rum Runner

One of my favorite beverages is rum. In fact, the main character in my novels, Doc Ford, is known to enjoy a few rum drinks during the sunset hour. —RWW

1½ ounces rum

½ ounce crème de banana

¼ ounce blackberry brandy

sour mix

grenadine

Place rum, crème de banana, brandy, a splash of sour mix, a dash of grenadine, and 2 ice cubes in a blender. Process until smooth and serve immediately.

SERVES 1.

Recipe courtesy of The Sanibel Grill at The Timbers Restaurant & Fish Market on Sanibel Island.

Tropical Breeze

A delightful cocktail from The Jacaranda on Sanibel. —RWW

¾ ounce Southern Comfort

¾ ounce Crème de Noyeaux (almond-flavored liqueur)

¾ ounce peach schnapps

¾ ounce blackberry brandy

3 ounces sour mix

slice of fresh orange

Place liquors and sour mix in a blender with ice and blend until smooth. Transfer to a hurricane glass and garnish with orange slice.

SERVES 1.

Recipe courtesy of The Jacaranda on Sanibel Island.

Week at the Beach

This delicious drink is from The Normandie at the West Wind Inn on Sanibel, just footsteps from a beautiful white sandy Gulf beach. —RWW

1 ounce vodka	pineapple juice
½ ounce apple schnapps	cranberry juice
½ ounce peach schnapps	slice of fresh orange
orange juice	

Fill a tall glass with ice cubes. Add vodka and schnapps. Add equal parts orange, pineapple, and cranberry juices to fill the glass. Stir and garnish with orange slice.

SERVES 1.

Recipe courtesy of The Normandie at The West Wind Inn on Sanibel Island.

Tropical Depression

This recipe comes from my friend Matt Asen, one of the great restaurateurs and chefs, and among my favorite traveling partners. —RWW

1½ ounces vodka	sour mix
½ ounce brandy	grenadine
½ ounce amaretto	1 ounce Coca-Cola
2 ounces pineapple juice	

Place vodka, brandy, amaretto, pineapple juice, a splash of sour mix, and a dash of grenadine in a shaker with 3 ice cubes. Shake to blend well. Pour into a tall glass and float the Coca-Cola on top.

SERVES 1.

Recipe courtesy of The Sanibel Grill at The Timbers Restaurant & Fish Market on Sanibel Island.

Cuba Libre

A popular Cuban cocktail with international popularity. —RWW

> 2 ounces Bacardi or Havana Club white rum
>
> juice of ½ lime
>
> cola
>
> lime wedge

Fill a highball glass with ice. Add rum and lime juice. Fill glass with cola. Garnish with lime wedge.

SERVES 1.

Recipe courtesy of Randy Wayne White.

Happy Hour at Tarpon Lodge on Pineland

The History of Rum in the Caribbean

Do you know why rum has always been associated with sailors and similar Caribbean travelers? It's because, in the tropics, stored fresh water quickly develops algae and becomes slimy. So the custom in the British Navy was to "sweeten" the ship's water supply with alcohol.

In 1655, Vice-Admiral William Penn (father of the founder of Pennsylvania) arrived in Barbados and captured Jamaica and an entire rum factory. For the frugal British Navy, rum became the alcohol ration of choice. In later years, the recipe ration was exactingly described in Admiralty Law: A quart of water was mixed with a half-pint of rum on deck and in the presence of the Lieutenant of the Watch. Sailors were given two servings a day: one between 10:00 a.m. and noon and the other between 4:00 and 6:00 p.m. To make it more palatable, it was suggested sugar and lime be added.

In 1756, the mixture of water and rum became part of the regulations, and the call to "Up Spirits" sounded aboard Royal Navy ships for more than two centuries thereafter. God Bless the Queen! —RWW

Cabbage Key Creeper

This unique blend of tropical fruit juices and island libations is Cabbage Key's signature favorite, guaranteed to help you settle into the island pace. Kamora is a rich coffee liqueur traditionally blended by the Mayan Indians. I've enjoyed many of these tropical favorites when visiting this historic property where Mary Roberts Rinehart once wrote. —RWW

  pineapple juice

  coconut milk

  1½ ounces Jamaican rum

  ¾ ounce Kamora or other coffee liqueur

Place pineapple juice and coconut milk in a shaker and stir to mix. Add rum and shake until frothy. Pour into a highball glass. Float coffee liqueur on top.

SERVES 1.

Recipe courtesy of Cabbage Key.

Jungle Juice

A delightful beverage to serve your friends from the North. —RWW

1¼ ounces Gran Gala or other orange liqueur

½ ounce Myers's dark rum

½ ounce banana liqueur

pineapple juice

orange juice

grenadine

slice of fresh orange

Fill a blender half full of ice. Add orange liqueur, rum, and banana liqueur. Add equal parts pineapple and orange juices but do not completely cover the ice with liquid. Add 1 dash grenadine and blend until creamy smooth. Pour in a tall glass and garnish with orange slice.

SERVES 1.

Recipe courtesy of The Normandie at The West Wind Inn on Sanibel Island.

Sunset over J. N. "Ding" Darling National Wildlife Refuge

My Panamaniac Friends

Among the closest friends I have in the world are my "Panamaniac" friends. They are men and women who were born, raised, went to school, and worked in the Panama Canal Zone prior to the final transfer of power. They are Zonians; a class and quality of people unto themselves. Because they grew up in the tropics of Central America, they live lives that are slower, but higher in sensuous quality than most. They are gourmets without snobbery; master cocktailologists without agendas. My Panamaniac friends include Captain Bob Dollar, who ran a tugboat on the canal, his gorgeous wife Mindy, Tom "T-Bird" Pattison, who worked in some capacity (or another) for the US Military, and many others such as Teresa, Mimi, Lucho, Jay, Priscilla, and the Amazing Vern. They have contributed collectively to the following recipes, and to my life.—RWW

The Pirate Bob

2½ ounces Silver Flor de Cana rum

splash of cola

slice of lime

Fill a highball glass with ice. Add rum and a splash of cola. Garnish with lime wedge.

SERVES 1.

Recipe courtesy of Randy Wayne White.

Mindy's Mojito

juice of 1 key lime

1 tablespoon simple syrup

8 sprigs of mint

2½ ounces Silver Flor de Cana rum

club soda

Place lime juice, simple syrup, and 1 mint sprig in a highball glass and crush. Add rum. Fill glass with ice and club soda. Decorate with mint sprig.

SERVES 1.

Recipe courtesy of Randy Wayne White.

Bird's Bajan

Mount Gay Eclipse rum

water

lime

Fill a highball glass with ice. Add rum, water, and a squeeze of lime. Garnish with a lime wedge.

SERVES 1.

Recipe courtesy of Randy Wayne White.

Tarpon's Chocolate Martini

My house in Pineland is situated on a Calusa Indian mound across the street from the Tarpon Lodge, a historic inn, where marvelous sunsets go hand in hand with cocktail time. —RWW

Stoli vanilla vodka

Godiva chocolate liqueur

chocolate syrup

Place Stoli vanilla vodka and Godiva chocolate liqueur in a glass in a 2-to-1 ratio. Layer glass with chocolate syrup. Shake and serve.

SERVES 1.

Recipe courtesy of the Tarpon Lodge on Pine Island.

Key Lime Martini

Another wonderful cocktail from the historic Tarpon Lodge. —RWW

¾ ounce of Stoli vanilla vodka

¾ ounce Tuaca Liqueur

pineapple juice

freshly squeezed lime juice

Place vodka and Tuaca in a shaker. Add pineapple and lime juice in a 3-to-1 ratio. Shake and serve in a sugar-rimmed glass.

SERVES 1.

Recipe courtesy of the Tarpon Lodge on Pine Island.

Frozen Pineapple Daiquiri

The pineapple is a marvelous fruit. It is even more delightful when mixed with rum.—RWW

½ cup ice

2 ounces Captain Morgan's Original
    Spiced Rum

½ ounce fresh lime juice

½ cup fresh chopped pineapple

1 small slice fresh pineapple

Place all ingredients in a blender and pulse until smooth. Garnish with slice of pineapple.

SERVES 1.

Recipe courtesy of Carlene Fredericka Brennen.

Bodwitch Point, Fort Myers Beach, with San Carlos Bay, Sanibel Island, in the distance

Captain Mark's Mojo Mojito

This recipe comes from my friend Danelio Arrante, the past curator of the Hemingway Museum outside of Havana. —RWW

12 fresh mint leaves plus 1 sprig

4 teaspoons raw sugar

1 lime, cut into quarters

1½ ounces white rum

7 ounces club soda

Place mint leaves, sugar, and 2 lime quarters in a tall glass. Crush mint. Pound with handle of a wooden spoon or a muddle to release juices or essence. Fill glass with ice. Add rum and club soda. Stir to mix mojito. Garnish with a lime wedge and a sprig of mint.

SERVES 1.

Recipe courtesy of Randy Wayne White.

Jell-O Shots

I can't think of a dumber way to waste good vodka than using it in Jell-O shots—which is why, at Tarpon Bay, we always used the cheapest potato-based rotgut we could find. At our weekly Friday-night parties, they were popular with the cheerful tourist-types, men and women on vacation who were very, very eager to have a good time. As Tomlinson might say: A Jell-O shot isn't a drink, and it's not pleasant. It's more like an investment in something that might be pleasurable. —RWW

1 (⅓-ounce) box tropical flavored Jell-O

1 cup vodka

Add 1 cup boiling hot water to Jell-O in a medium bowl. Stir until Jell-O is dissolved. Stir in 1 cup cold water and vodka and transfer to shot glasses.

SERVES 10.

Recipe courtesy of Randy Wayne White.

Enjoy food with as many people as you can. Share the recipes in this book, and you will be opening the door to friendships that may last you a lifetime. —Randy Wayne White

AFTERWORD

Water is a mirror until you learn to use it as a lens. Through Polarized sunglasses, the sea bottom was iridescent. Beneath and beyond me were green fields of turtle grass that were vein-worked by riverine trenches of deeper water and craters of sand. On a low tide, I could use those submerged creeks and rivers to cross the flats as if traveling a mountain road.

There are valleys and hills and ridges below me, too, where lives were being lived. Tunicates and sea hydroids and sponges flew past, in a blur. I spooked a school or redfish that angled away as a herd, pushing an acre of waking water. A stingray flapped off in an explosion so abrupt that I could feel the shock wave through the fiberglass of my skiff.

I stood for a while, then I sat behind the wheel in the heat and light, comfortable and alone, on the move.

—*Ten Thousand Islands,* Randy Wayne White

PHOTO CREDITS

Courtesy of Carlene Fredericka Brennen
vi, ix, x, xii, xvii, xviii, xx (bottom left), xxiii (bottom left & right), xxviii, 3, 8, 14, 17,19, 22, 25, 26, 29, 30, 31, 37, 38, 45, 50, 52, 54, 57, 59 (top & bottom), 62, 65, 69, 70, 76, 79, 80, 82, 89, 93, 95 (bottom), 99, 100, 106, 110, 114, 118, 121, 124, 125, 126, 132, 134,135, 136, 143 (bottom), 145, 146, 148, 149, 156, 160, 162, 164, 169, 174, 176, 179, 183,184, 188, 192, 200, 204 (top), 208, 210, 214, 224, 227, 230, 237, 239, 243, 247

Courtesy of Randy Wayne White
12, 15, 32, 43, 90, 120, 130, 161, 163, 196, 216, 232, 240, 246

Courtesy of the Nick Clements family
xx (top), xx (top & bottom right), xxiii (top), xxiv (top & bottom), xxvi (top & bottom), xxvii (left & right), xvii (right), 6, 80, 95 (top), 147, 159, 173, 198, 203, 204 (bottom)

Courtesy of J. N. "Ding" Darling National Wildlife Refuge, US Department of the Interior Fish and Wildlife Service Bureau of Sport Fisheries and Wildlife Service Bureau
iii, xvi

Courtesy of Captain Neville Robeson
41, 45, 112

Courtesy of Terry E. Brennen
56, 96, 228

Courtesy of Bob Swinker
75, 155, 169

Courtesy of Dr. Oram "Doc" Kline
127

Newspapers: *Islander Newspaper,* 68, 172. *Island Reporter,* iv, v. *Sanibel-Captiva Shopper's Guide,* XIV, 143 (top)

ACKNOWLEDGMENTS

We would like to thank Carlene's daughter, Shamlene "Shamie" Kelly, for her typing of the original manuscript. Her assistance on this book and her knowledge of the preparation of food was invaluable. This book could not have been completed without her help. We would also like to thank Carlene's husband, Terry Brennen, for his support throughout this project. And thanks to his children, Scott Brennen and Andrea Brennen, for their support. And to Terri Blackmore for her contributions and advice. A special thanks to Anne Bellew for her research and to Robin Calabrese for allowing us to access the Breeze newspaper's photo files and to the staff at the *Sanibel-Captiva Shopper's Guide, Sanibel Captiva Islander,* and the *Island Reporter* for their help.

A special thanks to good friend and editor Scott Martell for his pagination and editing of our original draft. We would like to thank Kevin Dill and Michael Gulnac for their proficiency in scanning the photographs. Their expertise in this field was greatly appreciated. We would also like to thank WGCU production manager Sherri Coleman for her assistance and support.

A special thanks to Carlene's good friend, Lynda Leonard-Boyce, the past co-owner of the Sanibel Café. Lynda's expertise in the world of food preparation along with her contribution of recipes and advice was a tremendous help. And to Ken Boyce for his enthusiasm. Also, a special thanks to Carolyn and Jay Mirowitz who helped in the proofing of this book and for their support. Thanks to Carlene's brother Bill Semmer and his wife Shirley for their support and help throughout this project, and to their son Billy and Carlene's goddaughter Katie for their kindness and suggestions. We would also like to thank members of the staff of Semmer Electric—Jan Arding, Sandy Bianchi, and Ayita Rainey—for their help and the use of their office equipment. A special thanks to Captain Henry Gore and his wife Tracey, who gave new meaning to the preparation of fresh-caught shrimp.

We would like to thank refuge manager Rob Jess and past deputy refuge manager Susan White of the J. N. "Ding" Darling National Wildlife Refuge on Sanibel Island for the use of aerial photographs and documents of Tarpon Bay.

Thanks to Captain Nick Clements, his wife Becky, his mother Molly Clements, and family, and to Captain Neville Robeson for their trips down memory lane. And a special thanks to the Sanibel-Captiva Islands Chamber of Commerce board and the past chamber director Steve Greenstein for their help, and for allowing us to reproduce recipes from *The Best of Sanibel and Captiva Islands*. We would also like to thank Carlene's sisters, Lorraine Baldwin, Joanne Semmer, Betty Hill, and niece Krissy Baker for their support and help with family recipes. And to the manager of Bonita Bill's Waterfront Café, Barbara Whatley, for her expertise on marina foods.

A special thanks to the talented editors, designers, and production staff at Globe Pequot Press who worked on the first edition of this book in 2006, and to the equally talented team who re-envisioned the book in 2013, including editors Amy Lyons and Lauren Brancato, production artist Melissa Evarts, cover designer Bret Kerr, and interior designer Nancy Freeborn.

I'd like to thank my sons Rogan and Lee Wayne for their help and support. They have also inherited my mother's love of Southern cooking. A special thanks to my brother, Dr. Dan White. His memories of our lives growing up in North Carolina and the sharing of our mother's family's recipes were greatly appreciated. His contribution to this book was invaluable. I'd also like to thank Wendy Webb who is the sunshine in my life.

Also a special thanks to all the restaurant proprietors and talented chefs who are mentioned throughout. This book could not have been completed without their contributions.

—Randy Wayne White and Carlene Fredericka Brennen

I have known Carlene Fredericka Brennen for more than a quarter of a century. I met her at Tarpon Bay Marina on Sanibel Island, during my first year there as a fishing guide. Carlene, a Florida native for most of her life was then divorced, a young single mother, struggling to start her own newspaper, determined to remain independent, true to her own vision of self. Over the next thirteen years at Tarpon Bay, she became a valued member of our small marina community, and we celebrated her consistent successes as enthusiastically as we admired her intellect, her humor, and her commitment to excellence. She loves Florida and her photographs in this book show it.

—Randy Wayne White

INDEX

Italicized page numbers indicate photos.

Acosta, José de, 86
Alaska Snow Crab Clusters
    Cooked in Beer, 207
alcohol. *See also* beer; drinks,
    alcoholic
    Dan's Sanibel Rum
        Cake, 211
    Shrimp Cocktail with
        Tequila Sauce, 124
Alfredo Sauce, 18
All-Crab Crab Cakes, 128
An American Traveler (RWW),
    139, *138*
Andrews, Jean, 86
appetizers
    Captain Beard's Addictive
        Guacamole, 37
    Casa del Fuego BBQ
        Shrimp, 201
    Cheese Straws, 32
    Deep-Fried Artichoke
        Hearts with Hot Mustard
        Sauce, 35
    Sandy Hook Cracked
        Conch, 36
    Shamie Kelly's Hot Crab
        Dip, 30
    Smoked Mullet Dip, 28
    "Spread a Little Joy" Hot
        Cheese Dip, 31
    Teriyaki Wrap-Ups, 33

Twice-Fried Plantains
    (Tostones), 34
Apple Cranberry
    Casserole, 163
Apricot-Raisin Granola, 9
Araujo, Jorge, xvii, 88–89
Arnett, Jane, 20
Arrante, Daniello, 244
Artichoke Hearts with
    Hot Mustard Sauce,
    Deep-Fried, 35
Asen, Matt, 236

Backus, Mili, 31, *31*
bananas
    Banana Leaf Snapper with
        Lime Cilantro Sauce,
        140–41
    Bananas in Paradise, 216
    Fresh Mango Yogurt
        with Blueberries and
        Banana, 212
barbecue cooking
    Casa del Fuego BBQ
        Shrimp, 201
    Charcoal Grilled
        Grouper with Mango
        Butter, 202
    Hickory Barbecued
        Ribs, 199
    Kabobs, 198
Batfishing in the Rainforest
    (RWW), xxviii, 113
Baum, Claire, 182, 206

Bayardo (Costa Rican friend),
    72–73
"B" Brothers Chili, 42
beans
    "B" Brothers Chili, 42
    Perfect Beans, 189
    Sue Gray's Sanibel Soup, 52
Beard, Scott, 37
beef
    "B" Brothers Chili, 42
    Brisket in Beer, 206
    Cabbage Key Cheeseburger
        in Paradise, 154
    Kabobs, 198
    Marinated Beef Strips, 150
    Ribs Jamaican, 152
    Sanibel Island Chili, 49–50
    Steak 'n' Mushroom
        Kabobs, 153
    Sue Gray's Sanibel Soup, 52
    Teriyaki Wrap-Ups, 33
    Tournedos Chasseur, 151
beer. *See also* drinks, alcoholic
    Alaskan Snow Crab Clusters
        Cooked in Beer, 207
    Brisket in Beer, 206
    Captiva Cajun Beer Batter
        for Shrimp, 207
    Favorite Beer Muffins, 13
    pig roast and, 197
    Sanibel Beer Buster, 233
    on Sanibel Island, *204*, 205
    travel adventures and,
        225–26

Belizean Chicken Stew, 40
Bern (cook), 72–73, 74
berries
    Cranberry Jam, 23
    Fresh Mango Yogurt with
        Blueberries and
        Banana, 212
    Jane Arnett's Island
        Marmalades and
        Jellies, 20
    Red Raspberry and Peach
        Jam, 24
    Strawberry Freezer Jam, 23
Berry, Paula, 201
The Best of Outside (RWW), 25,
    46, 93, 147
beverages. *See* drinks, alcoholic
Billheimer, Mike, 12, 18–19
Bird's Bajan, 241
Blackmore, Terri, 49, *50,* 60, 70
Bloody Mary, 228
Blueberries and Banana, Fresh
    Mango Yogurt with, 212
Bonita Bill's Salsa, 92
Boyce, Ken, 9
Brazilian Potato and Meat Pie
    (Nhoques de Forno), 172
Brazilian Tuna Omelet (Mal
    Assado), 10
Bread, Corn, 15
Breaded Pork Tenderloin
    Sandwich, 173
Brennen, Carlene Fredericka,
    47, 49, 52, *56,* 58, 70, *75,*
    81, *96,* 182, 206, *228,*
    234, 242
Brennen, Terry E., 31
Brine-Cured Pork, 158
Brisket in Beer, 206

Broccoli Casserole, 182
Broccoli Soufflé, 180
Broccoli Soup, 43
Broiled Florida Grapefruit, 11
Broiled: Florida Lobster, 131
Buffett, Jimmy, 154, *155*
Byers, JoAnn Wilson, *43,* 71,
    71, 187

Cabbage Key Cheeseburger in
    Paradise, 154
Cabbage Key Creeper, 238
Cakes
    Dan's Sanibel Rum, 211
    Old-Fashioned White
        Sheet, 215
    Texas Sheet, 217
Calamity Jane's Gazpacho, 44
Calusa tribe, 136
capsicums (hot peppers), 84–90
Captain Beard's Addictive
    Guacamole, 37
Captain Gene's Mullet, 142
Captain Mark's Mojo
    Mojito, 244
Captiva Cajun Beer Batter for
    Shrimp, 207
Captiva Cool, 13
Captiva (RWW), xix, 7, 27,
    39, 197
Carlene's Golden
    Margarita, 234
Carrots, Herbed, 78
Casa del Fuego BBQ
    Shrimp, 201
ceviche
    in Baja Mexico, 63–68
    Ceviche de Hotel
        Hemingway, 69

Dead Bern's Ceviche,
    72–73, 74
    and Paloma Magallanes,
        63–68
    Shrimp Ceviche, 71
Charcoal Grilled Duck with
    Raspberry Sauce, 168
Charcoal Grilled Grouper with
    Mango Butter, 202
Charlene (tarpon tournament
    winner), 75
cheese
    Brazilian Potato and Meat
        Pie (Nhoques de
        Forno), 172
    Cheese Straws, 32
    Cheesy Hash Brown
        Potatoes, 187
    Cheesy Potatoes, 183
    Sliced Tomato
        Genovese, 60
    "Spread a Little Joy" Hot
        Cheese Dip, 31
Cheeseburger in Paradise,
    Cabbage Key, 154
Cheesy Hash Brown
    Potatoes, 187
Cheesy Potatoes, 183
chicken
    Belizean Chicken
        Stew, 40
    Chicken in Coconut Soup
        (Tom Kha Gai), 46
    Chicken Romano, 167
    Chicken with Rice, 191
    Curried Chicken, 165
    Georgia Wilson White's
        North Carolina Fried
        Chicken, 161

Green Curry Shrimp
(as alternative
ingredient), 123
Guatemalan Juliana
Soup, 48
Kabobs, 198
Mesquite Grilled Chicken
with Herbed Wild Rice,
Apples, and Walnuts, 166
Nicaraguan Valencia Rice,
194–95
chili
"B" Brothers Chili, 42
Sanibel Island Chili, 49–50
chilies, 85–89
chili oil, 116, 117
chocolate
Easy & Delicious
Cookies, 219
Chocolate Pecan Pie, 217
Oreo Balls, 221
Tarpon's Chocolate
Martini, 242
Chowder, Conch, 47
chutneys
Mango Chutney, 94
Pineapple Chutney, 91
Citrus Vinaigrette, 56
clams
Clams Marinara, 107
Seafood Linguine with
Marinara Sauce, 108
Cocktail Sauce, 104
coconut
Coconut Island Pie, 210
Coconut Shrimp, 125
Columbus, Christopher, 86
conch
Conch Chowder, 47

Conch Salad, 70
Sandy Hook Cracked
Conch, 36
Consommé Rice, 193
cookies
Date Nut Balls, 223
Easy & Delicious, 219
Oreo Balls, 221
crab
Alaskan Snow Crab Clusters
Cooked in Beer, 207
All-Crab Crab Cakes, 128
Crab Cointreau, 127
Crab Puffs, 129
Sanibel Seafood Benedict
with Alfredo Sauce,
18–19
Seafood Linguine with
Marinara Sauce, 108
Shamie Kelly's Hot Crab
Dip, 30
Tarpon Bay Crab Salad, 61
Cranberry Casserole,
Apple, 163
Cranberry Jam, 23
Cuba Libre, 237
Cuban Death-Lift (RWW),
120, 221
Cuerve Gold Chili Team,
49–50, 50
curing meats, 157–58
Curried Chicken, 165

daiquiris
Doc Ford's Hemingway
Daiquiri, 232
Frozen Pineapple
Daiquiri, 242
Dan's Sanibel Rum Cake, 211

Dark Light (RWW), 105
Date Nut Balls, 223
Dead Bern's Ceviche, 72–73, 74
Dead of Night (RWW), 17, 63,
105, 201, 231
Deep-Fried Artichoke Hearts
with Hot Mustard Sauce, 35
The Deep Six (RWW), 73,
80, 204
Denson, Della Wilson, 14, 14,
185, 221
desserts
Bananas in Paradise, 216
Chocolate Pecan Pie, 217
Coconut Island Pie, 210
Dan's Sanibel Rum
Cake, 211
Date Nut Balls, 223
Easy & Delicious
Cookies, 219
Fresh Mango Yogurt
with Blueberries and
Banana, 212
Key Lime Pie, 213
Nuttie Fingers, 220
Old-Fashioned White Sheet
Cake, 215
Oreo Balls, 221
Sweet Potato Pie, 222
Texas Sheet Cake, 218
dips
Shamie Kelly's Hot Crab
Dip, 30
Smoked Mullet Dip, 28
"Spread a Little Joy" Hot
Cheese Dip, 31
Doc Ford's Captiva Rum Bar &
Grille, xvii, 122
Doc Ford's Captiva Sunrise, 231

Doc Ford's Fort Myers Beach
    Rum Bar & Grille, xvii,
    82, 122
Doc Ford's Hemingway
    Daiquiri, 232
Doc Ford's Island Mojito, 233
Doc Ford's Sanibel Rum Bar
    & Grille, xvii, 122, *149*,
    149–50
Dollar, Bob and Mindy, 240, *240*
"*Dr. Pepper*" (RWW), 90
dressings, salad
    Citrus Vinaigrette, 56
    Marinade, 110–11
    for Sliced Tomato
        Genovese, 60
drinks, alcoholic. *See also* beer
    Bird's Bajan, 241
    Cabbage Key Creeper, 238
    Captain Mark's Mojo
        Mojito, 244
    Carlene's Golden
        Margarita, 234
    Cuba Libre, 237
    Doc Ford's Captiva
        Sunrise, 231
    Doc Ford's Hemingway
        Daiquiri, 232
    Doc Ford's Island
        Mojito, 233
    Frozen Pineapple
        Daiquiri, 242
    Jell-O Shots, 244
    Jungle Juice, 239
    Key Lime Martini, 242
    Mindy's Mojito, 241
    The Pirate Bob, 241
    Randy Wayne White's
        Margarita, 227

rum, history of, 238
Rum Runner, 235
Sanibel Beer Buster, 233
Sanibel Slammer, 234
Sanibel Sunrise, 234
Tarpon's Chocolate
    Martini, 242
travel adventures and, 225
Tropical Breeze, 235
Tropical Depression, 236
Vodka-Oyster Shooters, 229
Walden Pond Bloody
    Mary, 228
Week at the Beach, 236
Duck with Raspberry Sauce,
    Charcoal Grilled, 168

eggs
    Brazilian Tuna Omelet (Mal
        Assado), 10
    Captiva Cool, 13
    Mexican Tomato Poached
        Eggs (Huevos
        ahogados), 16
    Sanibel Seafood Benedict
        with Alfredo Sauce,
        18–19
Easy & Delicious
    Cookies, 219
Everglades (RWW), 81, 92,
    133, 174, 209
Everglades Assault
    (RWW), 79

Favorite Beer Muffins, 13
fish. *See also* shellfish
    Banana Leaf Snapper with
        Lime Cilantro Sauce,
        140–41

Brazilian Tuna Omelet
    (Mal Assado), 10
Captain Gene's
    Mullet, 142
Ceviche de Hotel
    Hemingway, 69
ceviche in Baja Mexico,
    63–68
Charcoal Grilled Grouper
    with Mango Butter, 202
Creole Grilled Grouper,
    Hearts of Palm Salad
    with, 56–57
Dead Bern's Ceviche,
    72–73, 74
Flounder Baked in Spicy
    Tomato Sauce, 139
Grilled Grouper Wrapped
    in Prosciutto on Bed of
    Salsa, 98
Grilled Marinated Shark
    Fillets, 137
Grilled Shark of Lake
    Nicaragua, 135
Grouper Dijon, 146
Herb-Grilled Grouper, 81
mullet, description of, 27
Pan-Seared Pompano with
    Summer Marinara
    Sauce, 144
sharks, information on, *132*,
    134, 135, 136, 137
Smoked Mullet Dip, 28
Florida Lobster, Yellow-Tomato
    Gazpacho with Medallions
    of, 131
Flounder Baked in Spicy
    Tomato Sauce, 139
Fresh-Cooked Shrimp, 116

Fresh Mango Yogurt with
    Blueberries and Banana, 212
frosting, cake, 216, 217
Frozen Pineapple Daiquiri, 242
fruit
    Apple Cranberry
        Casserole, 163
    Bananas in Paradise, 216
    Broiled Florida
        Grapefruit, 11
    Charcoal Grilled Grouper
        with Mango Butter, 202
    Coconut Island Pie, 210
    Coconut Shrimp, 125
    Cranberry Jam, 23
    Fresh Mango Yogurt
        with Blueberries and
        Banana, 212
    Frozen Pineapple
        Daiquiri, 242
    Jane Arnett's Island
        Marmalades and
        Jellies, 20
    Red Raspberry and Peach
        Jam, 24
    Seagrape–Key Lime
        Jelly, 22
    Strawberry Freezer Jam, 23
    Tropical Fruit Salsa, 97
    Twice-Fried Plantains
        (Tostones), 34
    Watermelon Jam, 21

garlic, 78
garlic butter, 137
Gatrell, Tucker, 7–8
gazpacho
    Calamity Jane's
        Gazpacho, 44

Yellow-Tomato Gazpacho
    with Medallions of
    Florida Lobster, 53
Georgia Style Candied Sweet
    Potatoes, 185
Georgia Wilson White's
    Creamed Onions, 186
Georgia Wilson White's North
    Carolina Fried Chicken, 161
glaze, cake, 211. *See also* icing,
    cake
A Gold Medallion (RWW), 203
Gore, Henry, 126
Gone (RWW), 45, 71
Graeme (marina manager), xxi,
    xxii, *xxiii*, xxv, *29, 146*
Graham, Maggie, *228*
Grand Cayman Siam (RWW),
    186, 193, 213
Grapefruit, Broiled Florida, 11
Gray, Sue, 52, *228*
Green Curry Shrimp, 123
Grilled Grouper Wrapped in
    Prosciutto on Bed of
    Salsa, 98
Grilled Italian Vegetables, 178
Grilled Marinated Shark
    Fillets, 137
Grilled Shark of Lake
    Nicaragua, 135
grouper
    Charcoal Grilled Grouper
        with Mango Butter, 202
    Creole Grilled Grouper,
        Hearts of Palm Salad
        with, 56–57
    Grilled Grouper Wrapped
        in Prosciutto on Bed of
        Salsa, 98

Grouper Dijon, 146
Herb-Grilled Grouper, 81
Guacamole, Captain Beard's
    Addictive, 37
Guatemalan Juliana Soup, 48

Hamilton, Gene, 142
Hanselman, Galen, 64–68
Harder, Patrick, 60
Hearts of Palm Salad with
    Creole Grilled Grouper,
    56–57
The Heat Islands (RWW), 55,
    101, 149, 190
Hemingway, Ernest, 232
Herbed Carrots, 78
Herb-Grilled Grouper, 81
herbs, cooking with, 77–78, 81
Hickory Barbecued Ribs, 199
hot sauces, 83–90
Hot Sauce Team, 90
Huevos ahogados (Mexican
    Tomato Poached Eggs), 16

icing, cake, 216, 217. *See also*
    glaze, cake
An Island Off Borneo
    (RWW), 167

jalapeños
    Bonita Bill's Salsa, 92
    Mango Chutney, 94
    origin of, 87
    Tropical Fruit Salsa, 97
jams and jellies
    Cranberry Jam, 23
    Jane Arnett's Island
        Marmalades and
        Jellies, 20

Red Raspberry and Peach
Jam, 24
Seagrape–Key Lime Jelly, 22
Strawberry Freezer Jam, 23
Watermelon Jam, 21
Jane Arnett's Island
Marmalades and Jellies, 20
Jell-O Shots, 244
Joyce (marina cook), xix, xxv,
xxvi, 116, 117, 119
Joyce's French-Fried
Shrimp, 119
Joyce's Marina Grilled
Shrimp, 117
Jungle Juice, 239

kabobs
Kabobs, 198
Steak 'n' Mushroom
Kabobs, 153
Kelly, Shamie, 30, 49, 50
Kershen, Brian, 110–11, 123
Key Lime Martini, 242
Key Lime Pie, 213
key limes. *See* limes and key
limes
Key West Connection
(RWW), 223

Lamb, Rack of, 175
Last Flight Out (RWW),
68, 90
Lee, Bill "Spaceman," *196*
Leonard-Boyce, Lynda, 9, 22,
23, 25, 51, 78, 91, 109, 127,
139, 178, 183, 207, 210
limes and key limes
Carlene's Golden
Margarita, 234

Key Lime Martini, 242
Key Lime Pie, 213
Lime Cilantro Sauce, 140
Seagrape–Key Lime Jelly, 22
lobster
Broiled: Florida Lobster, 131
Seafood Pasta Salad, 58
Yellow-Tomato Gazpacho
with Medallions of
Florida Lobster, 53

Mack (marina proprietor), xx,
xx, xxi, xxii, xxv, xxvi, 197
Magallanes, Paloma, 63–68
Mal Assado (Brazilian Tuna
Omelet), 10
mangoes
Fresh Mango Yogurt
with Blueberries and
Banana, 212
international festivals for, 94
Mango Butter, 202
Mango Chutney, 94
Tropical Fruit Salsa, 97
The Mangrove Coast (RWW),
21, 141, 178, 205
The Man Who Invented Florida
(RWW), 7–8, 156, 164, 229
margaritas
Carlene's Golden
Margarita, 234
Randy Wayne White's
Margarita, 227
Marinara Sauce, 108
Marinated Beef Strips, 150
Marinated Mussel Mini-
Brochettes or Salad, 110–11
Marmalades and Jellies, Jane
Arnett's Island, 20

martinis
Key Lime Martini, 242
Tarpon's Chocolate
Martini, 242
Matthiessen, Peter, 5
Mayeron, Victor, 129, 213
McRae, Jewel Wilson, 32, 216,
229, 223
meals, tradition of, 1, 4, 5
meats, curing and smoking
techniques for, 157–58
meringue, 222
Mesquite Grilled Chicken with
Herbed Wild Rice, Apples,
and Walnuts, 166
Mexican Tomato Poached
Eggs (Huevos
ahogados), 16
Mindy's Mojito, 241
mojito
Captain Mark's Mojo
Mojito, 244
Doc Ford's Island
Mojito, 233
Mindy's Mojito, 241
Muffins
Mindy's Mojito, 241
Favorite Beer, 12
Pecan Pie, 14
mullet
Captain Gene's Mullet, 142
description of, 27
Smoked Mullet Dip, 28
Mushroom Kabobs,
Steak 'n,' 153
mussels
Marinated Mussel Mini-
Brochettes or Salad,
110–11

Seafood Linguine with Marinara Sauce, 108
Mustard Sauce, Deep-Fried Artichoke Hearts with Hot, 35

Nayrilla's Corn Bread, 15
Nelson, Greg, 141
Nhoques de Forno (Brazilian Potato and Meat Pie), 172
Nicaraguan Valencia Rice, 194–95
Nick (marina employee), *xx,* xxi, xxii, *xxiv,* xxv, *xxvii, 159*
North of Havana (RWW), 157
Nuttie Fingers, 220

Old-Fashioned White Sheet Cake, 215
Onions, Creamed, 186
Oreo Balls, 221
outdoor cooking
    Casa del Fuego BBQ Shrimp, 201
    Charcoal Grilled Grouper with Mango Butter, 202
    Hickory Barbecued Ribs, 199
    Kabobs, 198
oysters
    in New Orleans, 102–3
    Oyster Cocktails, 104
    Oysters Creole, 105
    Scalloped Oysters, 103
    Vodka-Oyster Shooters, 229

Panamaniac friends, 240, *240*
Pan-Broiled Veal Chops, 171

Pan-Seared Pompano with Summer Marinara Sauce, 144
Pasta Salad, Seafood, 58
Pattison, Tom "T-Bird," 240, *240*
Payne, Alex, *173*
Peach Jam, Red Raspberry and, 24
Pecan Pie Muffins, 12
Penn, William, 238
peppers, hot, 83–96
Peppers: The Domesticated Capsicums (Andrews), 86
Perfect Beans, 189
Perfect Hot Sauce, 83–90
Perfect Rice, 190
pies
    Chocolate Pecan Pie, 217
    Coconut Island Pie, 210
    Key Lime Pie, 213
    Sweet Potato Pie, 222
Pig Roast and Beer Cotillion, 197
pineapples
    Frozen Pineapple Daiquiri, 242
    Pineapple Chutney, 91
The Pirate Bob, 241
Plantains, Twice-Fried (Tostones), 34
Pompano with Summer Marinara Sauce, Pan-Seared, 144–45
pork
    Brazilian Potato and Meat Pie (Nhoques de Forno), 172
    Breaded Pork Tenderloin Sandwich, 173

Brine-Cured Pork, 158
curing and smoking, 157–58
Grilled Grouper Wrapped in Prosciutto on Bed of Salsa, 98
Hickory Barbecued Ribs, 199
Ribs Jamaican, 152
Sanibel Island Chili, 49–50
potatoes
    Brazilian Potato and Meat Pie (Nhoques de Forno), 172
    Cheesy Hash Brown Potatoes, 187
    Cheesy Potatoes, 183
    Georgia Style Candied Potatoes, 185
poultry. *See also* chicken
    Charcoal Grilled Duck with Raspberry Sauce, 168
    Sue Gray's Sanibel Soup (turkey), 52

Rack of Lamb, 175
Rainey, A.L., 92, 94, 142
Randy Wayne White's Margarita, 227
raspberries
    Raspberry Sauce, 168
    Red Raspberry and Peach Jam, 24
Rawlings, Marjorie Kinnan, xi
Red Raspberry and Peach Jam, 24
Remoulade Sauce (for All-Crab Crab Cakes), 128

Remoulade Sauce (for Captiva
    Cajun Beer Batter for
    Shrimp), 207
Ribs Jamaican, 152
rice
    Chicken with Rice, 191
    Consommé Rice, 193
    Nicaraguan Valencia Rice,
        194–95
    Perfect Rice, 190
Robeson, Neville, *41, 45, 112*
rum. *See also* drinks, alcoholic
    Dan's Sanibel Rum
        Cake, 211
    history of, 238
    Rum Runner, 235
Russo, Johnsie Wilson, 163,
    163, 193

salads
    Conch Salad, 70
    Hearts of Palm Salad with
        Creole Grilled Grouper,
        56–57
    Marinated Mussel Mini-
        Brochettes or Salad,
        110–11
    Seafood Pasta Salad, 58
    Sliced Tomato
        Genovese, 60
    Tarpon Bay Crab Salad, 61
salsas
    Bonita Bill's Salsa, 92
    Grilled Grouper Wrapped
        in Prosciutto on Bed of
        Salsa, 98
    Tropical Fruit Salsa, 97
Salt-Curing Meat in
    Brine, 157

sandwiches
    Breaded Pork Tenderloin
        Sandwich, 173
    Cabbage Key Cheeseburger
        in Paradise, 154
    Sandy Hook Cracked
        Conch, 36
    Sanibel Beer Buster, 233
    Sanibel Flats (RWW), xv, 94,
        107, 152, 159, 225
    Sanibel Island Chili, 49–50
    Sanibel Island Cuervo Gold
        Chili Team, 49–50, *50*
    Sanibel Seafood Benedict with
        Alfredo Sauce, 18–19
    Sanibel Slammer, 234
    Sanibel Sunrise, 234
sauces
    Alfredo Sauce, 18
    Cocktail Sauce, 104
    Hot Mustard Sauce, *35*
    hot (peppers), 83–90
    Lime Cilantro Sauce, 140
    Marinade, 110
    Marinara Sauce, 108
    Raspberry Sauce, 168
    Remoulade Sauce (for All-
        Crab Crab Cakes), 128
    Remoulade Sauce (for
        Captiva Cajun Beer
        Batter for Shrimp), 207
    Summer Marinara
        Sauce, 144
    Tequila Sauce, 124
    Teriyaki Marinade, 137
Scalloped Oysters, 103
scallops
    Scallops Provençal, 109
    Scallop Stew, 51

Seafood Pasta Salad, 58
Schlosser, Wil, 234
seafood. *See* fish; shellfish
Seafood Linguine with
    Marinara Sauce, 108
Seafood Pasta Salad, 58
Seagrape–Key Lime Jelly, 22
Shamie Kelly's Hot Crab
    Dip, 30
shark
    Grilled Marinated Shark
        Fillets, 137
    Grilled Shark of Lake
        Nicaragua, 135
    kayak fishing for, 136, 138
    photographs, 132, 135
    selection and preparation
        of, 135
Shark River (RWW), 77, 115,
    177
"Sharks from a Kayak" (RWW),
    136, 138, 139
The Sharks of Lake Nicaragua
    (RWW), 102–3, 133–34,
    170, 200
shellfish. *See also* fish
    Alaskan Snow Crab Clusters
        Cooked in Beer, 207
    All-Crab Crab Cakes, 128
    Broiled: Florida Lobster, 131
    Captiva Cajun Beer Batter
        for Shrimp, 207
    Casa del Fuego BBQ
        Shrimp, 201
    Clams Marinara, 107
    Coconut Shrimp, 125
    Conch Chowder, 47
    Conch Salad, 70
    Crab Cointreau, 127

Crab Puffs, 129
Fresh-Cooked Shrimp, 116
Green Curry Shrimp, 123
Joyce's French-Fried
    Shrimp, 119
Joyce's Marina Grilled
    Shrimp, 117
Marinated Mussel Mini-
    Brochettes or Salad,
    110–11
Oyster Cocktails, 104
Oysters Creole, 105
oysters in New Orleans,
    102–3
Sandy Hook Cracked
    Conch, 36
Sanibel Seafood Benedict
    with Alfredo Sauce, 18
Scalloped Oysters, 103
Scallops Provençal, 109
Scallop Stew, 79
Seafood Linguine with
    Marinara Sauce, 108
Seafood Pasta Salad, 58
Shamie Kelly's Hot Crab
    Dip, 30
Shrimp Ceviche, 71
Shrimp Cocktail with
    Tequila Sauce, 124
Shrimp Perlo, 126
Tarpon Bay Crab Salad, 61
Tarpon Bay Shrimp, 120
Vodka-Oyster Shooters, 229
Yellow-Tomato Gazpacho
    with Medallions of
    Florida Lobster, 53
shrimp
    Captiva Cajun Beer Batter
        for Shrimp, 207

Casa del Fuego BBQ
    Shrimp, 201
Coconut Shrimp, 125
cooking techniques for, 116
Fresh-Cooked Shrimp, 116
Green Curry Shrimp, 123
Joyce's French-Fried
    Shrimp, 119
Joyce's Marina Grilled
    Shrimp, 117
Seafood Linguine with
    Marinara Sauce, 108
Seafood Pasta Salad, 58
Shrimp Ceviche, 71
Shrimp Cocktail with
    Tequila Sauce, 124
Shrimp Perlo, 126
Tarpon Bay Shrimp, 120
Sliced Tomato Genovese, 60
Smoked Mullet Dip, 28
smoking meats, 157–58
snacks. See appetizers
Snapper with Lime Cilantro
    Sauce, Banana Leaf, 140–41
soups and stews
    "B" Brothers Chili, 42
    Belizean Chicken Stew, 40
    Broccoli, 43
    Calamity Jane's
        Gazpacho, 44
    Chicken in Coconut Soup
        (Tom Kha Gai), 46
    Conch Chowder, 47
    Guatemalan Juliana
        Soup, 48
    Sanibel Island Chili, 49–50
    Scallop Stew, 51
    Sue Gray's Sanibel
        Soup, 52

Yellow-Tomato Gazpacho
    with Medallions of
    Florida Lobster, 53
"Spread a Little Joy" Hot
    Cheese Dip, 31
squash
    Grilled Italian
        Vegetables, 178
    Summer Squash
        Casserole, 181
Steak 'n' Mushroom
    Kabobs, 153
Strawberry Freezer Jam, 23
Sue Gray's Sanibel Soup, 52
Summer Marinara Sauce, 144
Summer Squash Casserole, 181
Sweet Potato Pie, 222
Sweet Potatoes, Georgia Style
    Candied, 185
Swinker, Bob, 49

Tampa Burn (RWW), 27, 192,
    195, 218
Tarpon Bay Crab Salad, 61
Tarpon Bay Shrimp, 120
Tarpon Fishing in Mexico and
    Florida (RWW), 150
Tarpon's Chocolate
    Martini, 242
Ten Thousand Islands (RWW),
    14, 19, 247
tequila. See also drinks,
    alcoholic
    Carlene's Golden
        Margarita, 234
    Randy Wayne White's
        Margarita, 227
    Shrimp Cocktail with
        Tequila Sauce, 124

Teriyaki Marinade, 137
Teriyaki Wrap-Ups, *33*
Texas Sheet Cake, 218
tomatoes
    "B" Brothers Chili, 42
    Bonita Bill's Salsa, 92
    Calamity Jane's
        Gazpacho, 44
    Grilled Grouper Wrapped
        in Prosciutto on Bed of
        Salsa, 98
    Hearts of Palm Salad with
        Creole Grilled Grouper,
        56–57
    Mexican Tomato Poached
        Eggs (Huevos
        ahogados), 16
    Shrimp Perlo, 126
    Sliced Tomato Genovese, 60
    Tropical Fruit Salsa, 97
    Yellow-Tomato Gazpacho
        with Medallions of
        Florida Lobster, 53
Tom Kha Gai (Chicken in
    Coconut Soup), 46
Toolan, Dan, 9, *50,* 211, 234
Tostones (Twice-Fried
    Plantains), 34
Tournedos Chasseur, 151
"A Train, America and a Frog"
    (RWW), 102–3

travel and food, 4–5
Tropical Breeze, 235
Tropical Depression, 236
Tropical Fruit Salsa, 97
turkey
    Sue Gray's Sanibel
        Soup, 52
Twelve Mile Limit (RWW),
    83, 197
Twice-Fried Plantains
    (Tostones), 34
"The Twig Syndrome"
    (RWW), 147

veal
    Pan-Broiled Veal Chops, 171
vegetables
    Broccoli Casserole, 182
    Broccoli Soufflé, 180
    Cheesy Potatoes, 183
    Georgia Style Candied
        Potatoes, 185
    Georgia Wilson White's
        Creamed Onions, 186
    Grilled Italian
        Vegetables, 178
    Herbed Carrots, 78
    Kabobs, 169
    Perfect Beans, 189
    Summer Squash
        Casserole, 181

Sweet Potatoes, Georgia
    Style Candied, 185
Sweet Potato Pie, 222
Vinaigrette, Citrus, 56
Vodka-Oyster Shooters, 229

Walden Pond Bloody
    Mary, 128
Watermelon Jam, 21
website, author's, 90
Week at the Beach, 236
White, Dan, 1–5
White, Georgia Wilson
    (author's mother), 1–4, 161,
    161, 218, 219
White, Rogan, *196*
Williams, Lamar, 207
Willie (marina boat manager),
    xxi, xxii, xxv, *xxvi*
Wilson, Nayrilla, 15, *15,* 222

Yellow-Tomato Gazpacho
    with Medallions of Florida
    Lobster, 53
Young, K. S., 92, 94, 142

zucchini squash
    Grilled Italian
        Vegetables, 178